Look What God Can Do

Linda Lee Greenhalgh, age six. She survived to tell all who would listen of the goodness of God.

Lynne Stevens

ISBN: 979-8-9851748-0-9
eBook ISBN: 979-8-9851748-1-6

Library of Congress Control Number: 2022910016

Edited by Sandra Wissinger
Cover image by Helena Bosse
Ebook Conversion by Amit Dey

Printed in the United States of America
First Printing October 2022
Published by Lynne Stevens, Owls Head, Maine
www.LookWhatGodCanDo.com

Good News

Contents

Acknowledgements

Father, Jesus, and Holy Spirit were always there for me during the dark times and the light. They never left me. They were faithful. They brought about as much change and healing as I was able and willing to receive. I love my incredible Creator. The purpose of this book is first and foremost to honor and thank Him.

I love my parents very much. It could be said that this book is as much from their hearts as it is from mine. I thank my earth father and mother, Cy and Marge Greenhalgh, who with me came to make a difference in the lives of incest survivors and to bring an awareness of the goodness of God. It was not easy for any of us.

I thank my sister, Jo, who knew that something wrong was happening to me and tried to help me. She was also there for me in later years when I struggled.

I thank my incredibly wonderful children, Bailey Smith and Heidi MacMillan, who were my reason to keep going. They have always been there for me through good times and tough times.

I thank my husband, George Stevens, who was worth the wait.

I thank The Rev. Canon Andrew Miller, LCSW, (aka Andy Miller) for his pioneering healing work with dissociation and abuse. He is good, kind, and beloved by many.

I thank Dr. Robert Berube who was our family counselor and wise person. He knew far more than I realized.

I thank Tineke C. Vandergrift, Psy.D., a wonderful Christian counselor who really listened to me. She offered hope and healing in the early days of my journey towards wholeness.

I thank Dottie Egan, a wonderful counselor who helped me move past anger as a response to life.

I thank Susan F. Seeber, Lic.Ac., who with her needles and cups, years of education, and sensitivity, brought much healing and friendship.

I thank Nancy Duprey, Connie Messer, and Peggy Moore of Faith Worship Center for their years of experience with the Sozo lay ministry, their willingness to work with me, and all the mentoring and healing they brought into my life.

I thank Pastors Daryl and Lin Nicolet who founded Faith Worship Center. There I became a born again Christian and found God's love, people, guidance, and transformation. It was Daryl who spoke the salvation prayer over me.

I thank Faith Worship Center (FWC), Pepperell, MA, for being a place of love, worship, healing, prayer, friendship, learning, and Truth, a place that is truly heaven on earth.

I thank Steve Cummings for finding me at the pool at the Westford Regency Inn where with his son he prayed over me and suggested FWC as a church to attend when I said I wanted to be a healer.

I thank Jonathan and Cindy Gale and Paul and Leslie Gosselin for their love and friendship. They mentored me for many years at their home group. It doesn't get better than that!

I thank Randy and Irene Lagios for their love and friendship over many years at home group. Irene gave me a Bible and a hymnal when I first attended FWC. She also loved on me when I needed it, which was often.

I thank Leslie Russell for her love and friendship. She was my small group advisor during my second year of Faith School of Supernatural Ministry (FSSM). I appreciate her for helping me survive a very dark divorce.

I thank Joyce Graves: friend, spiritual mother, prayer warrior, and whatever else I needed her to be as I made the transition over the years from a very needy new Christian to one of God's kids.

I thank Walter Niederberger for his friendship, prayers, and comfort in times of great need. I admire his devotion to the Lord. He exemplifies a true spiritual warrior and follower of Jesus. His faith moves mountains!

I thank Bob and Carol Snoddy for their love and friendship and for times of deep healing at their lovely home.

I thank Victoria Ann, Victoria Levesque, Christy Monahan, and Hanna DeHoff for their ministry of therapeutic massage. Their hands-on healing worked wonders in my life.

I also wish to thank my beloved pets for their unconditional love and the joy and comfort they brought me. These include three American Cocker Spaniels—Bentley Smith, Matthew Theodore Smith, and Buddy Smith—and four cats of mixed breed—Mittens Greenhalgh (childhood cat), Aristotle Smith, and Aslan Osgerby and Prince Caspian Osgerby (both Maine Coon cats and brothers). I look forward to seeing them in heaven.

Preface

Note to the Reader:

This is a book about love—the love of God for His children. He is restoring my life at age seventy-nine after many trials. If He can restore my life, He can restore yours.

> Jeremiah 29:11
>
> "For I know the plans I have for you," declares the LORD, "plans to prosper you and not to harm you, plans to give you hope and a future." (NIV)

I spent many years uncovering and healing from the events of my childhood. I prayed and asked God to open a window to my childhood so I could write my story with His knowledge, wisdom, and clarity. The Holy Spirit responded and gave me much of the material I've included. I took notes when Holy Spirit ministered to me during times of deep healing. The Holy Spirit has written this book with me. God brought me through it all, and to Him goes the ultimate credit. This is truly His book. I am so very thankful for the goodness of God. I want the whole world to know that He is available for them too.

With God all things are possible. This book has taken a lifetime to write and many people to help me along the way; for them I am eternally grateful.

It is important for me to mention that much of what I have written here is hard to read. It is hard for me still. Skip Part One if you need to and begin at Parts Two and Three. There is much of value throughout the entire book with respect to healing that I am eager to share with you.

Be blessed.

Acknowledging My Parents:

The three of us: Mom and Dad and me.

I want to honor my father who was such a wonderful provider for his family of seven. I had an abundant life as a child. I did not want for food, shelter, clothes, lessons, or advantages. With my mother he purchased an estate-like lodge on a beautiful lake and then did all the maintenance so that his wife and girls could have a place to swim. He did not have a chance to swim as a child, and I only saw him go in the water once. He was a lion of a man and ahead of his time.

I have many fond memories of him. As a child I would listen to tales of his hobo days during the Great Depression when he and his brother rode the rails to make money to help feed their family. Later, when I was a cheerleader, he did not make me wear boots on the bus when it snowed and that meant a great deal to me. He attended all our recitals and concerts. As a grown woman I so loved our talks into the night after my long drive with my two Cocker Spaniels from work in Massachusetts to camp in Enfield, Maine. He waited up for me even though it was often late. He was gallant.

I want to honor my mother who brought up five daughters with love and common sense. She had excelled in school and obtained a degree in home economics. She taught school before her marriage to my dad. Later in life, she taught piano lessons in their home and then took a master's degree in education and taught second grade. She was a wonderful cook, incredibly creative in her endeavors, and ahead of her time—a modern woman who read to us about life. She sewed for us and made sure we got music and dance lessons and could be involved in as many activities as we wanted. She taught Sunday school and took us to church with her. We went to the library on Saturday and returned home with dozens of books. She loved family activities and planned many parties and gatherings.

My mother put a lot of thought into how to raise each one of us. She became a wonderful mother to me once I left home. And she was a wonderful grandmother and great grandmother. We eventually became best friends. She prayed for us when we needed praying, and it was **her** prayers for me that got me to God.

Acknowledging My Sister:

I treasure this figurine of sisters called "Telling Her Secret" that my sister, Jo, gave me many years ago. I dearly love my sister! She has done her best to counsel and care for me. She was so much better than I knew. I have no idea what it was like for my sister growing up, but I do know that she was always there for me, especially when I was a teen and later raising my children. She listened to me still later when I called crying on her shoulder through some of life's trying times; I so appreciate and love her.

Hummel Goebel Telling Her Secret #196/0 – 1948.

Look What God Can Do

Part One: What Happened to Me

How I was badly hurt from before I was born until I left high school. God was always with me and cared for me often in ways I didn't see or acknowledge until much later.

Part Two: How God Healed Me

God had a plan for my life and found a way to direct me back to it by taking my job! My desperation sent me to Faith Worship Center where God began to restore my life and get me back to that wonderful plan.

Part Three: The Goodness of God

It is impossible to overstate the goodness of God. He is WITH us. He is FOR us. He LOVES us

Part One: What Happened to Me

How I was badly hurt from before I was born until I left high school. God was always with me and cared for me often in ways I didn't see or acknowledge until much later.

1. Introduction

As a young woman, my mother wanted to get away from her mother and fell in love with my father. They married and she became pregnant with me. At some point she realized he had a real problem. She knew that once she had me, she would be stuck with him. She went as far as going to a witch woman to get something to abort me from the womb, but it didn't work. I first experienced her rejection in the womb, and I had no place to run. Needless to say, my welcome to planet earth was not a good one.

When my mother became pregnant with a second child, she reconciled herself to a life with my father. He did not hurt me until the baby came. Something changed when my mother had her second child. She felt fulfilled as a mother. She actually liked this baby and found herself cooing over her. As a two-year-old, I watched and felt unloved. I was *not* loved by my mother, not at all.

My mother did a terrible thing—I will tell all. She gave me to my father for his use in order to protect my baby sister. People say young children don't understand what is happening, but I certainly did. I had rage in my heart when she did this. I saw her face when she did that, and I saw a look that said, "*You* take it for a while." My father started hurting me soon after my sister came, so I connected the two events: her coming to live with us and my father hurting me—badly.

There would be no onlookers in the morning, so before the birds started their singing, my father would get me out of bed to rape me. He touched my quivering body with reverence and awe as if there were something holy about it. I was terrified.

He did not seem like the man my father was but someone so different—stern, hard, and unyielding. I would scream, so he tied my mouth shut and tied my hands together. Once he was finished, he seemed disgusted with me as if I were of no account. He left me and I trundled off to bed to try to get some sleep before the day started.

I felt sick and unclean, and I did not understand who this person was who seemed to be masquerading as my father. He was bad man to me and no real father. I hated him with a passion and did not know why my mother honored him, respected him, and kowtowed to him.

Me with my dolly at seven years old.

I hated my mother too as she was not like a real mother to me, only showing affection to my baby sister. She took care of me and tended my wounds, but no lovingness ever came out of her toward me as long as I lived in their home.

I lived a double life. I had this life of my father hurting me in the middle of the night and this life of playing with my neighborhood friends who were mostly boys. My neighborhood friends and my sister and I built a playhouse together on my parent's property in Connecticut. It was my haven, my favorite place of joy to be with my friends and to be safe. I was safe at school too. It was only there that when I lay down to rest from our play and learning, *I was safe*.

Me age five hard at work creating something of beauty with a neighborhood friend Fall 1947.

Even as a toddler, my sister knew that I was being hurt and that something bad was happening to me. She tried to help me as best she could. When I was four, my two-year-old sister and I tried to escape by running away with some pennies she had found. My father caught us, and in response, burned down our little fort/playhouse.

My father dragged me into our home by my hair up the stairs and gave me the thrashing of my life. He broke bones and when he was done, I looked like I had been in an automobile accident. My mother put me in the back room close to the kitchen and tended my wounds, but she showed me no loving kindnesses. Jesus came and tended to my spirit and gave me the chance to leave the planet, but I chose to stay. No doctor came to tend to my wounds; I just lay on the bed—alone.

My friends saw what happened to me, and they told their parents. It was another time then, when parents "owned" their children, so there was nothing they could do to help me. I was sorry that my friends now knew what I was dealing with—at least on a physical level—at home. My friends and Jesus kept me alive. He ministered to my spirit, and slowly my body recovered. My heart and mind were sorely afflicted by what happened when my father burned down our little playhouse. Something changed after that. My sister got no punishment of any kind for our little break toward freedom, but now I was being watched for what I might do.

My mother, my little sister, and me possibly off to the beach a few minutes from home.

My mother let me go down to the beach alone from a very early age. Her thought was that someone would always be there for me,

4

but that was not always true. I walked the beach with a heavy heart and tried to figure out what to do. All I knew was that someone had called me a pretty little girl; so, I decided from then on, I would be ugly. I screwed up my face and scowled at the world whenever I could manage it. I loved my time at the breach because I was away from my mother who hated me. How could a woman hate her child so?

Unfortunately for me, my dad did not show or tell my mom how much he loved her until much later in their lives. He cooed over me. He couldn't help it. He had grown up with five other boys and was delighted to have a girl child as the first child. My mother was terribly jealous and took it out on me. She pulled my hair when she was braiding it. She hit me hard on the face to show her displeasure when he wasn't around. She put my nose in my bowel movements in order to train me. She was not a loving mother to me, and she spoke word curses over me: that I would never marry and would be ugly always.

My mother and father were just too much for me to bear. I remember kneeling down by the side of my bed as a small child to have a heart-to-heart with God. I told Him that He was my God and I was His child, and I was not happy with the life He had provided. I asked Him to please come and get me and give me a different assignment. I waited and waited and waited some more.

I then confronted God about how I was being hurt over and over, asking Him why this was my lot in life. I truly believed God the Father would come in person to rescue me or at least send a flock of angels to remove me from this hell hole. He did not come to save me, and believe me I was very angry with God. If it didn't work to pray and ask, what else could I do? I would just have to stick it out. I was a young child who had never known any kind of love or kindness and was totally and unalterably fed up.

Asking God for help didn't work. I had already tried making myself ugly to keep my father off me. That didn't work either. So, I settled in and did the very best I could with the life that I had. I had a place to live. I had two parents one of whom hated and hurt me and the other who seemed to care for me at times but then hurt me terribly. I never made any sense out of my life until much later.

Me at age seven making mud pies in Spring.

2. Early Life

My father was one of six smart rambunctious boys in a family that had roots in Scandinavia. His dad had had a difficult life and was bitter over any good that happened to come to the life of one of his sons. He was an entrepreneur and full of ideas about how to make enough money for them to have the life he wanted for them. That he didn't succeed as well as he wished was deeply troubling for him.

Their family home had burned to the ground. There was a bucket brigade using pails of water, but it was not enough soon enough to save the house. After that, they never returned to the kind of life they had before. My dad's dad took all his boys except the youngest to work the family silver mine. It was hard work and required them to go underground for long hours. They worked the mine as a family and there was enough money from mining for my dad to go to college and earn a master's degree in mining engineering. He was very good at getting things to work: as a child he had to fashion things out of whatever material was at hand. He had a wonderful mind, loved playing bridge, and was larger than life. He was a handsome man who wore leopard skin in the family photo albums. Later in life, he joined a writing club and wrote and published a fascinating book about his life entitled *Rogues, Hoboes, and Entrepreneurs: Coping With The Great Depression*[1].

---

[1] Cy W. Greenhalgh, *Rogues, Hoboes, and Entrepreneurs: Coping With The Great Depression*, (: 1st Books, 2000)

His mother was good and kind. She baked five or six loaves of bread every day. (Her boys were hungry!) She bought truckloads of vegetables from her sister and brother-in-law who farmed the land and then the family put them by to eat over the winter.

My dad's mom had been a teacher with a philosophic frame of mind who later in life spoke in public against the perils of war and the virtues of peace. My dad's mom loved her husband, but she knew he had a terrible dark side.

My dad's father had been particularly cruel to my dad when he was a young boy. He had hurt him physically and sexually by putting foreign items into his anus. He caused my father to become a child with two sides: one side good and one side dark.

After that happened, my father never knew when the dark side would break through. He learned he had to watch himself always to keep himself on the good side. In general, that strategy worked well unless (when he got older) he had something alcoholic to drink. Drinking alcohol allowed the dark side to come out. It was the dark side of my good father that hurt me so badly. The good side did not know what the bad side did. It wasn't until my father was in his seventies that he even had an inkling of the terrible things he had done. I don't think he ever fully came to grips with what he had done. My father is in heaven now, and for that I am grateful.

My father also had a real problem with anger. He would have to run out of the house so as to deal with his anger in ways other than by killing me. He couldn't stand to hear me cry when I was a baby. I believe my crying triggered him to another time when his dad hurt him, and my dad's rage was really directed against his father. At any rate, the one who got hurt was me, not my father's father. He couldn't help himself. The anger would come unbidden, and he would take it out on me. When he realized what he was doing or when my mother alerted him to what he was doing, he would rush out of the house terribly distressed with himself.

I cried loudly at times because my mother fed me by the clock and not by my appetite. My mother got better at mothering with my younger sisters; but as a new mother with me, her oldest, she timed my bottles at four hours. Her discipline taught her not to feed me before the clock indicated it was time. I cried to no avail. We lived with my father's parents for a time, and his mother held me and rocked me to comfort me since no milk would be provided until my mother provided it.

When I was a little older, either one of my parents would put a bandana over my mouth; cover my eyes; tie my wrists, knees and ankles together; and put a rope around my body. They would put me in a utility closet so as not to rouse my father's ire. If I could have seen my guardian angel in that closet with me, I would have been comforted. But I did not, and I spent many unhappy times tied in the closet.

I was terrified: I thought I was going to die. I lost circulation to my hands and feet; my feet became flat blobs that seemed like swirling paddles. I didn't know what I had done wrong or how long I would be left there. I knew that my mother had intervened on my behalf and that my father had been about to hurt me. I sometimes saw him run away so as not to hurt me. My mother left me there until it was safe to take me out. She did not show me any tenderness when she came for me; I was a chore to her, but she did not want me to die.

There seemed no hope for me. There was no place to turn and no one to ask for help. Now there are telephone numbers you can call to ask for real help, but that was not the case when I was a child. At about four years old, I put my emotions away in an old trunk for safe keeping. It was not safe to be me, and it was not safe for me to feel because I might act out of my feelings. I had to be careful at all times or I could be murdered.

What was it like to grow up as a child with no emotions? Life was DULL. In some ways I did not feel alive. I was alive, but I did not feel alive. There is a big difference. Over time my emotions became "frozen." Having frozen emotions probably saved my life.

My little sister was cared for; I was not. Life was good, but mine was not. There was much that didn't make sense to me. My father, for example, made no sense. There were times he cooed over me and told me he loved me. Other times, he turned into a monster and hurt me so badly I didn't know if I could endure it. He was both good and bad, okay and not okay, handsome and hideous. And why did he persist in touching me in ways that were NOT OKAY with me?

Me in my new snowsuit nineteen months old at Thanksgiving in 1943.

I spent a lot of time trying to understand why my little sister did not get the same abusive treatment I got. I don't think I thought it was her fault, but it surely did not seem fair. She and my mother were very close, and I was certainly the "odd man out." I was experiencing hell on earth. I had asked God to take me out of my hellish existence, but He had evidently refused because I saw little improvement in my life.

I was, however, fortunate to have had two beautiful places to get away to with very little motherly attachment to pull me back. I spent as much time as possible either at the field next to the house or at the beach walking back and forth. Had I known Jesus then—known that God was with me in the form of the Lord Jesus Christ—it would have been such a comfort. Sadly, I was probably too angry to notice Him!

I surely had a problem with anger. It seemed that everywhere I looked, my anger was provoked! I saw everything as a child. I noticed that a lot of parents seemed unlikely candidates for the care of their precious young ones. People hurt one another with their words and actions; and children had few, if any rights. I railed at much. Little children love their parents despite how they treat them. I loved my parents very much and did not understand why I should be so badly treated.

Parents don't seem to realize that their children do not belong to them. Their children are on loan from God. Parents are supposed to be role models for their children and, at the very least, provide loving homes for them. I didn't see much—if any—of that kind of attitude. I felt like Cassandra (one who knows but is not believed), and I was just a little child trying to make sense of the world.

My message to the world is this:

Parents, your children have feelings, and they are very much aware of how your behavior affects them. Children love their parents; that is just the way it is. Parents, you need to be worthy of their love.

My mother was unhappy in her marriage and the only thing she had control over was me. She hit me in the stomach when I was an infant, crossed my legs, and then tied the nightgown so I couldn't kick. She force-fed me and even tried to drown me. Fortunately for me, Jesus persuaded her to have a change of heart and not believe the lies from the dark side that she would be better off without me.

My mother did not like being a mother. She managed us girls with iron discipline. We both did what she said as best we could so as not to get her ire going. I didn't see her angry with my sister, but she used the same unloving mothering skills with her as she did with me. She raised the two of us as she was raised—with a firm hand. She didn't know how to love a child with easy ways. Her style as a mother was hard and unyielding.

I had a mind of my own, and she would have preferred a rag doll. I cried vigorously and often well before the appointed time for food, and I would not stop. It became a battle of wills. She would not feed me before the scheduled time, and I would not be quiet. She did not like me because I didn't do what she expected.

She was disciplined and methodical in the preparation of my bottles and caring for my physical needs, yet she would tie my hands when she did not want me to use them. Later, when I got poison ivy, she tied my hands at night before bed and put vile tasting nail polish on my nails so I could not bite them. She would also restrain me by tying the bottom of my nightgown. That upset me terribly, and I cried loudly. She had power over me, and she was not judicious in exercising it. She didn't mean to hurt me, but I certainly got hurt.

I was a problem for her. She didn't want me in her life. In another time, she would have sent me off to a governess. She did not care for the chores associated with caring for a baby and she longed to be free from those duties. Her mother had not been a loving mother, and so she had no role model.

There was something between us that was not healthy. For one thing, I thought I knew better than she how a mother should care for a child, and she did not care for me in that way. Instead, she took out all her personal problems on me. I was somewhat miserable. I felt that I had to fend for myself. I steeled myself to this at a very young age. For some unknown reason I was different, uncared for, alone in a troublesome world.

My sister didn't seem to cry as vigorously as I did, and she got what she wanted and needed and I did not. It made me angry. I couldn't help it, but I was very jealous. I wanted the kind of affection my baby sister got, so I hated my sister. Life was not good for me. Yes, I had a roof over my head and nourishing food; but I was not loved, and I didn't understand why. My mother was quite unhappy except for the time she spent with my sister. They had a very special connection, and that is just the way it was.

My mother had issues with my father who was not loving and kind to her. They loved each other, but were woefully unaware of how to make each other happy. Her husband was supposed to be hers exclusively, and he wasn't. My dad did not give my mother the loving affection she craved from him. He gave it to me. He liked me very much and was ecstatic to have a girl child after growing up in a household of boys. When he was gone, she would slap me across the face—never enough to leave a mark, but enough to take her anger out on me.

Later in life, I realized that my father did love my mother, but he was not demonstrative. His father had not shown his mother how he felt about her, so he had no model for loving. He did not know how to give my mother the kind of love she craved, and she did not know how to show him how to love her. He would have been willing to learn as long as she did not guide with criticism. The problem was that all they both knew was criticism, and criticism was not a good teacher. I believe that if my father had just been loving to my mother or if she had been able to understand that sometimes these things happen or if she had spoken up with him, things might have been different. But it was not to be.

I wanted to be loved! I wanted somebody to love me. I felt totally unloved by my parents. My guardian angel was with me always, but I couldn't see it at the time. Jesus was always with me, but I didn't

13

know how to look and sense His presence. I know now that sometimes when little children are so terribly hurt, they hold themselves together and don't know how to accept what is available to them. It was a good thing I had the strength of Job—because I needed it.

Me age four in my new Easter outfit on Easter of 1946.

I lived in fear all the time. I never knew when things would happen, so I lived on guard at all times. I became stoic accepting that times away from home were safe and times at home were not safe. I didn't know what to do. The part of my father that loved me would have never hurt me. That other part came out and did things he seemingly had no control over.

3. The Razor Strap

Lots of times when I went to bed as a small child I didn't know if I would wake up the next morning. I lived in terror. I used to run and hide in the closet when my father came home from work. He beat me on a regular basis. I learned to spend as much time outside as possible to forestall the beatings.

Back then children didn't really have rights. No one checked me over for bruises. I didn't talk about it with my neighborhood friends. It was something to hide and not tell anyone. I would wear long sleeves to hide the bruises, and I stayed out of school when it was too obvious. My mother helped me with the hurts that I got.

My father beat me with his belt and hurt me physically. He had no remorse. He hit me with the belt buckle and on my face. I was seven or eight years old and protesting being raped. I remember the look on my father's eyes when he beat me with his belt. He had rage, and it had nothing to do with me. I was always afraid of my father. I thought I was a bad child.

I held my painful feelings inside. Some of them got trapped in my hands, a fact I learned much later in therapy. A kind therapist taught me how to talk to my fingers and hands and tell them I loved them and that they were useful and needed for more than as a repository for hurt, sad feelings.

A razor strap is a thin flexible strip of leather used to sharpen a straight razor. My father used his razor strap on me. He hit me where he felt like hitting me or all over the body. Sometimes he strapped

15

me down. Sometimes he held me with one hand and hit me with the other. I was terrified he would kill me.

At school. I am in front with braids and a scowl. Why did no one notice I needed help at home?

No one ever came to help me, but Jesus was always with me. I didn't know how to call on Him. I thought there was something terribly wrong with me to cause my father to hurt me so. My mother took my sister in another room when he hit me and attended to my bruises when it was over. I learned to keep my mouth shut because the beatings were worse when I cried. I stuffed the screams and the tears inside. And the anger went inside too. I didn't know how to escape the beatings except to play outside until real late and to stuff the angry sad feelings instead of expressing them.

My mother left me to deal with this side of my father and busied herself with household matters. When she bandaged and helped me there was no sympathy or love or compassion. It was like being fed to the dogs. I was the fresh meat. My father left my mother and my sister alone after he had beaten me. My mother and sister took it for granted that I would be hit. Fresh meat for the dogs is an expression intended to convey what the bad side of my father needed. Like a dog who eats a large slab of meat every night the bad side of my father needed a regular dose of hurting me to be satisfied. This part of my father was connected to Satan's kingdom.

4. The Burning of our Fort

Our neighborhood fort as we were building it. I am pointing at the fruit of our labor.

I had wonderful friends. I think they were mostly boys except for a few girls and my sister who tagged along as best she could. I did not want her there because I blamed her for stealing my parents from me. We played in the field next to my house and we whooped it up yelling and running around.

Look! See? There is a butterfly, a white one—probably a moth flitting here and there. Let's chase it a while, watch it a while—anything away from home that was glorious and good.

My friends were my raison d'être, my reason for living. They loved me, and we played well together. It didn't matter that I was a girl; I was one of them. I have always liked being with boys and men. I loved playing with dolls, but it seemed that boys had more fun.

18

Girls did dishes and cleaned house, and that wasn't my thing. Boys got to think and do something that counted for something. We played house. We played farm. We did tag and ring around the rosy.

My six-year-old birthday party; I am the one with braids, no hat, and the big smile.

Life in Westport, Connecticut continued. Westport was a charming little community. My mother was friendly and had time on her hands. She planned gatherings for neighborhood groups and exercised her cooking skills. She used her creativity as a hedge against the hard edges of my father.

My father was at work as a metallurgist in Bridgeport during the day generally happy with his job. He loved playing bridge at lunch. My dad had a wonderful mind, curious and able, and he loved to have a good time. Work was a good place for him.

I didn't like my sister. She did not get abuse from either parent. It was most unjust in my eyes. I could find nothing to like about her. She was the apple of my mother's eye but ugly in mine. I sought to keep her from my circle of neighborhood friends, and to some extent I was successful. She was better than I was willing to see. She knew I was being hurt and didn't know how to help me. Remember the pennies she found so I could escape?

My parents didn't realize how much hope I had set on that small journey to freedom. The deck was stacked against me. I had no resources, no local friendly person to help me. I felt totally alone in all the world. I became stoic as a way to cope. I was very angry with God. I had heard that God was in charge of the world, and I didn't understand how a God could be so mean. I was a very angry child— neither parent loved me, there was no justice and seemingly no escape from the terrible world I inhabited.

On a typical day like any other, my mother, father, sister and I were eating breakfast in the kitchen. My dad left for work whistling and happy to go. My mother braided my hair and did my sister's hair. She sewed, cooked, or cleaned.

Suddenly, there I was standing with Jesus holding my hand watching my freedom burn to the ground. My dad burned down our neighborhood hideout in front of my friends, told me he would burn me inside it if I ran away again, held my feet to the fire, then dragged me up the front steps by my hair and gave me the worst beating of my life. Now all my friends saw what my father was like and how I was treated at home. Now everyone knew my shame. My friends did not desert me; they told their parents, but back then no one interfered with a parent's upbringing of their child.

I felt as if my life were over, and I knew I would get a terrible beating. I did not expect the fury with which my father beat me. He could hardly wait to get me in the house before he began to hurt me and throw me around. He called me an ungrateful wretch. I had more than he had, and I had the nerve to believe that the grass would be greener somewhere else. Didn't he provide me with a good home? Didn't I have a roof over my head? Didn't I get fully fed with all the vital nutrients? What was wrong with me? Didn't I get how fortunate I was to be living with him and his good wife? What a nerve I had. And corrupting my little sister. All the bad things that had ever happened to him rushed through his mind, and he knew that I had it good whereas he had it very hard. Why didn't I appreciate what I had?

The flames seemed to fill the sky. My friends were nearby playing when they somehow got word that my father was up to no good. They had heard that my sister and I had tried to run away and had been found and brought back. They could see that my father was beside himself with rage that the two of us had tried to leave home. Why he had never considered such a move for himself, and he was a boy whereas my sister and I were merely girls. And he had something to run away from whereas I had a privileged home in the country with two parents and all the accoutrements of a good life. What a nerve I had. And for certain it was my fault, not that of my little sister. And you needed to be punished for having the gall to believe you could leave your parents by choice.

My mother and sister got out of the way. It was not safe to be around my father. He was beside himself with yelling and screaming. I was terrified. I did my best to hold myself together so as not to make it worse. When his fury was spent, he left the house and my mother carried me to a room on the first floor of our cottage and did what she could to attend to my wounds. I was in bad shape; I looked like I had been in an accident. She did not take me to the doctor or a hospital or call the police. She was afraid of my father and did what she could to stay out of the way when he got mean.

Jesus gave me a choice: to live or to die. I did not die because I chose to live. I told God that if I lived to grow up, I would help others who had been terribly hurt like I was. There is so much pain in the world. I thought my life was over. I was terrified. I didn't know parents could do that to their children. I was afraid. I was so terribly afraid. I didn't know Jesus would stay with me. I thought I was alone in all the world and that nobody loved me. I was on my own and I didn't know what to do. I was so afraid.

Words cannot describe how I felt. I was in utter despair for my life. I did not know if I would live after the beating my father gave me. I did not know if my friends would ever speak to me again. I had done my best to hide the despicable behavior of my parents from my friends, but now the truth was out. I was lower than low.

21

My mother was left to minister to my wounds and broken bones, and she was none too pleased with me. She had her own issues and taking care of my bruises and bandages and bodily functions was not what she would have liked to do with her time. She did not really have compassion for me; she took care of me in a mechanical way without love. I was always there now, and she had less freedom when I needed attention. I saw my hope vanish as I watched the fort vanish in front of my eyes. And I believed that my father would burn me in another fort if I ever tried to leave again.

The burning of the fort was a turning point between my parents and me. I had less freedom, and now I was being watched. Things hardened between us. I still played with my friends, but now they all knew my shame and how I was treated at home. Whereas before I had hidden the terrible truth, now everyone knew. It was very difficult for me because I was so sensitive to how others saw me. My sister and I did not talk about it. She knew that I was badly beaten, and she got no punishment. She did not know how to help me.

Among my neighborhood friends I had a kind of honored place that I did not really want. My friends all knew that I had been badly beaten because I did not come out for quite a while, and I was quite sober when I got back to life. Jesus had been ministering to my spirit. I didn't really know it was Jesus, but I responded and made the choice to live. My belief was that somehow, I would get free from my tormenters. I longed for love and believed I was unlovable and that there was something terribly wrong with me.

My solace was my friends—who admired my pluck—and my time of ramblings especially on the beach. I had real peace on the beach by myself. Others wondered whose little girl I was because they would not have let a child go by herself. I did a great deal of child thinking there and fortunate I was that I had a special place to go. I have always found a way to nurture my spirit by getting away to a wild place in nature. Even five minutes in such a place allowed me to survive a less than wonderful life. I loved to play in the field next to our house even though it was full of poison ivy. I felt free to run and play and be myself unfettered from the restraints of having to constantly monitor my surrounding for my safety.

Me at five and a half; so much sadness.

My life continued with little improvement. I was part of a family true. And I had shelter and clothing and food. But there was precious little love for me and an example in front of my face daily of my mother loving and caring for my sister. I had dark anger about it, and I hit my sister; I couldn't help it. I never understood the family dynamic except to know that she got love and I got anger and beatings. It was not fair in any way.

My mother saved my life when my father tried to beat me to death. I had run away from him because I didn't want to be hurt, but he grabbed me and dragged me inside up the front steps by my legs. My friends saw him dragging me and I was mortified. He then dragged me through the front room into the back room where he started to beat me to death with the butt of his rifle. His father had hurt him very badly, and he was taking it out on me. My mother got a small gun and came to the door. She told him if he didn't stop, she would put a bullet through him. I was badly hurt, and there was blood everywhere. My mother didn't dare take me to the doctors, so she cared for me herself. I didn't go out of the house for quite a while. Jesus never left me. I might not have made it without Jesus' ministering to my spirit. My strength came from Him.

I went to a school and there I was quite safe. Nobody ever questioned my absences or bruises. My bruises were bad. I took it like a stoic who believed that somehow someway it would get better. But it didn't ever until I went to college, and then I was free of them. I believe that when I left, one or more of my sisters might have been targeted, but I don't really know. None of them has ever said a word to me about abuse of any kind, so I am hopeful they were spared.

It's hard to believe, but I would eventually become best friends with my mother. After I left home, my mother tried to make it up to me the rest of her life. My mother was a good woman, and I loved her dearly.

5. Count on it. Go to God. He is so GOOD!

For years I had dark visions of two wolf-like creatures, one larger than the other, that came to my crib and took me out of it and away for their own use. I carried fear for years because of it. I had thought that these two creatures were my parents, but they were not.

A friend of my father stayed with us for a short time on his way back home on return from his time in the service. He had jumped as a paratrooper behind enemy lines. His experiences behind enemy lines traumatized him to no end.

He had been captured and tortured behind enemy lines, and he took out his rage on me. My father and his friend tortured me sexually. They used a small knife and other sharp implements. They lit a match on my crotch just to see how much pain it would give me. They burned my legs with matches. They didn't set me on fire; they just wanted to see how much pain they could inflict. They licked me and then threw me on the floor.

I think my father and his friend were holding hands. There was something wrong with the way they looked—they looked like animals and they looked sick. A therapist I consulted much later thinks his friend—like my dad—was hurt as a child. She said my dad and his friend were split off from reality and didn't even see that I was a baby; they thought they were back experiencing their own abuse.

25

How do I know? I had nightmare after nightmare about the experience, and the nightmare was confirmed much later through the words of God's Holy Spirit. It was the worst of all the horrible things that happened to me. I was a baby with no life experience to help me. The torture was excruciatingly painful and took many sessions of spiritual therapy to remove as much as was possible of the residue out of my psyche. I am so very grateful to God and to His healers for saving me from a lifetime of living under the mental and emotional consequences of the agony of that time. I had to forgive my father and his friend and ask God to bless them in order to leave that experience with the God who loves us all.

God was always with me through the dark times and the good. There were lots of good times for me. I loved being at the beach walking back and forth. I know that I agonized there, but I also appreciated the wildness of God's creation. I'm not sure I thought of it that way when I was four. I do know I loved the ocean, the wildness of it, the everchanging aspect of it. I suppose all of us look at the ocean and find whatever we want there: peace, distance from our problems, a sense of the presence of God's magnificent creation.

I tried to stay away from home as much as possible. Staying away did help. Later in life, when I was in junior high and high school, I signed up for all the outside activities possible so I would be away from home. I also realized after a time that staying quiet rather than yelling or screaming was better for me in that I got hurt less. Somehow the more I screamed the more the man masquerading as my father enjoyed hurting me.

I have worked very hard to forgive my parents and my father's friend and have peace in my heart. I truly love my parents and believe that they were involved as they were to enable me to get the word out that God is good. He loves each and every one of us and wants the best for us. A person's best way to solve a problem is to get on their hands and knees and reach out to their heavenly Father. In time He will respond. COUNT ON IT! GO TO GOD! HE IS SO GOOD!

6. Life in Maine

When I was about seven years old, we moved to Orono, Maine. My dad had taken a position as vice president and general manager at Old Town Pulp Products, Inc. in Old Town, Maine. I attended school in Orono from then until I graduated as a senior from Orono High School. I wish I could tell you that my father stopped hurting me after we moved, but it is not true. When I was a little older, he burned my legs with cigarettes.

There was an old iron bed to which he tied both my arms and my legs; then he put things—even a rifle—inside me. It hurt me very badly. He also covered my mouth so my screams would not be heard by the neighbors. He kept track of how long it took for me to show pain. He wrote it down in a little book and monitored my pain level. I learned to put my mind somewhere else so I wouldn't be so present with the pain. It was a game for him, but for me it was terribly distressing and worrisome. I never knew what he would devise next to hurt me. I don't think this happened too many times, but as many times as it happened was too many. My mother couldn't help me, and the doctor who examined me many years later thought I was a slut.

It was terrible. The reason I have such a passion against animals being experimented on in the lab is because of what my father did to me. He kept careful records of how much pain it took to make me cry, how much pain it took to make me scream, how much pain it took to make me pass out. I carried the terror for years—the terror of being badly hurt. He used the belt on me and beat me until I bled and begged for mercy. He put a broom handle inside me. He burned my bottom and thighs and crotch systematically with cigarette butts. The experiments, the beatings, the burning of my body, the stretching of my insides left deep emotional scars. He hurt me in every way imaginable: physical, emotional, mental, sexual. I was deeply wounded on all levels. One therapist who worked with me told me that truly I was hardy; another would be in a wheelchair and crippled.

Third grade eight years old.

God was always with me although I was mostly unaware. I don't remember that I ever told anyone about what happened with my father. I was terribly ashamed. There was NO PLACE TO GO, NO

28

ONE TO TELL, NO NUMBER I COULD CALL AND GET HELP. GOD WAS SUPPOSED TO BE MY HELPER, BUT I COULDN'T SENSE HIS PRESENCE OR HIS LOVE. It would have helped me so much. I was good. I was smart, fun-loving, and musical. I was helpful and kind and grew up believing that it was all about the other person, that I didn't matter much.

I always liked to get away on my own to little wild places. Many years later when I worked as a computer programmer I would walk to a little place with water, cattails, frogs, birds, trees—NATURE, a little wild place to rejuvenate myself and get ready for an afternoon of mind work. Oh, how I loved my little wild places. No one ever knew why or where I went, but I needed that wilderness of *the real world* to cope with my job. So much peace flooded my soul that I could return to work with a big smile on my face ready to dive into whatever lay ahead. It was my lunch time, and I ate of real joy.

The little hut with the old organ was a find near the camp of a family friend. I don't think I ever asked if I could play the old organ, but play it I did. I was quite a precocious child without drawing attention to myself. What I could have done with my life had my childhood been different. (I have such deep sadness that has not yet left me when I have such thoughts.)

One time I was happily enjoying playing the organ, and my dad came to me and took all his clothes off. He wanted me to suck his penis; and when I wouldn't, he started hitting me hard. But then he heard a sound and decided he had better retreat. That night he whipped me so hard I thought I was going to die.

When I was about fifteen, we moved to another home in Orono. I believe dad designed it. It had an intercom that allowed mom to speak to and listen in on all the rooms, a kitchen designed to suit mom's creativity with cooking and sewing, a playroom downstairs with a fireplace, and a Steinway piano in the living room. We all took lessons of all sorts. I got piano lessons, violin lessons, dance lessons, and voice lessons. Mom and dad were generous and wanted their girls to do well. It was a happy home with lots of comings and goings. It's true! Friends loved to come. We could walk, bike, or take the bus to school. I loved school. It was a sanctuary of sorts for me with friends and learning and best of all distance from my father whose activities were never totally foreseeable. I never knew when he would turn into that other guy who hurt me so terribly.

Sixth grade, age 11, 1953.

My parents bought an estate at Cold Stream Pond, Enfield, Maine when I was in middle school. It had substantial lake frontage on the pond, a beach of its own, a boathouse, a three-car garage complete with treasures, a basket factory, guest house, pump house, well, and an enormous lodge with five bathrooms and two wrap-around porches. There was a concrete water fountain in the front yard and a circular driveway. Oh, there was much scope for the imagination!

My father had been looking for a place for the Girl Scouts and found this spot. The Girl Scout management in town did not want the upkeep responsibilities, so he bought the lodge for his family. It was to be the place of happy memories, but first we had to clean it. Its former owner had run into hard times, and I believe sold it to dad "as is."

On one Saturday my mom and I were sorting odd, strange, and unusual canned and bottled delicacies in a pantry in the basement.

We were basically unloading all the shelves into the trash so we could dust and sweep cobwebs and filth from years of lack of attention. Suddenly my father appeared and pulled down his pants to rape me in front of my mother. She tried to stop him, but he had murderous intent. I told my sisters to run, and they did. I don't know what happened after that; but somehow, we all survived for another day.

Camp was a haven for all of us. Cold Stream Pond is a wonderful place to swim, and we had a great beach in front of camp as long as the water level of the pond was low enough. My mother encouraged her girls to invite friends to come to camp, and we did. My parents also invited friends, and there were many happy times with homemade peppermint ice cream and hot milk sponge cake with brown sugar frosting. My mother was the best cook of all time! She had been a home economics major, and she loved to create in the kitchen. She had not been allowed the privilege of much cooking in her home of origin as her mother was frugal. My mom made her kitchen and ingredients available to all of us girls, and my next younger sister and I especially liked to make waffles to serve our parents in bed and chocolate cake with chocolate frosting. At home, she kept a big freezer stocked with homemade cookies—especially chocolate chip cookies, and most of her daughters found their way to the cookies. (She must have wondered where all the cookies went.)

I only remember one other unhappy event at camp. I avoided going down to the basement which was large and dark and filled with many paint cans and tools for the upkeep of the camp. One time dad found me in the changing room, a small room with an outside door where we changed our clothes before and after swimming. We all changed in that little room, even my mom, and left our street clothes hanging on pegs.

Dad came into the changing room after I had taken my clothes off, and I saw the look in his eyes. I had not ever known him to enter that room as I only saw him swim once. I thought that room was a safe place. It was not that day. Almost as soon as it started, he heard

31

my mother calling for me, and he put his penis back where it belonged and took his hand off my mouth. He told me he would kill me if I ever told anyone. I had nightmares for weeks afterward and cried myself to sleep. What had I ever done to deserve such treatment? I was a good child and did everything I could to be helpful to each of my parents. It was so terribly sad.

I thought I was safe in our simple changing room. That that was not the case opened the realization I was never truly safe no matter where I was. My father could show up and hurt me at any moment. This belief became a stronghold in my life that undergirded me and kept me longing for true safety most of my life. Now at 79, I am truly safe with my Christian husband in the home he built in Owls Head, Maine. I believe that safety is a basic human need, and it needs to be met so as to provide a platform for a human life.

My father was totally in control; I had no choice in the matter, no options of any kind. He called me "kitten." The fellatio started at a young age. I was too small to give my father much pleasure, so he used my mouth. He went in my mouth. He used his tongue all over me, and he bit me. I'm willing to tell all! "Get your God damned cock out of my mouth, you bastard."

He bragged about his sweet meat with his mill buddies when he was drunk. He knew it was wrong. He would come into my room with his t-shirt on and carry me into the kitchen. He put me on the table and got behind me. I screamed and screamed, and no one came. He whacked me to shut me up. He was not at all loving. My mother did nothing; she was powerless to help me. My dad told me that he would blow my head off if I told or wrap me in a blanket so I couldn't breathe or see and put me on the street and run over me with a car.

My mother was a practical woman. She gave me a diaphragm as a gift on the first day of first grade. I can still see the douche kit. It was small and baby blue and white striped. I didn't use it; I threw it in the woods. It made me madder than hell. Not only was my father

32

raping me, my mother acknowledged and condoned it.

I remember my mother always asking me if I had my period. She kept track of my periods and when I was late, she had a fit. I was "having sex" with my father; I might get pregnant. That would cause a scandal and wouldn't be good for the family.

My father did get me pregnant at about age twelve. My mother was beside herself and as far as she was concerned, it was all my fault.

It didn't last long because my mother did not want a scandal. She tied me to a tree in the back yard and beat the pregnancy out of me with a piece of garden hose. I bled a lot. And then my father raped me while I was bleeding to show who was in control. I was devastated to have the baby taken from me. I had so little love in my life I desperately wanted a baby to love. Much later I realized it would have been bad for me and for my life to have had a child at twelve, but at the time I was close to inconsolable.

7. I am a Survivor

My mother believed that my father would murder us all if she left him. I am certain she was right. He was possessive, jealous, angry, and proud. We were all dependent on my father for survival. He had all the power: the job, the money, and a gun case full of guns.

I survived two group rapes. The first time I was about eight years old. My father brought home some men from the mill. They had been hunting. I tried to keep my father from coming in because he had a rifle, and he was drunk. He told me he would put the rifle up my crotch and shoot me if I interfered.

One of the three men slumped in a corner. My father walked around with his pants off. My father goaded the other man. I had no clothes on.

My father put his face in my crotch and licked and bit me. He was an animal in the wild with a delicacy that was still living. My father was on all fours. His eyes were red. The other man and dad rolled around with me getting high on the body contact. And then they wanted in.

I went and got the sewing scissors and tried to kill my father. I would have if I could have. He put the rifle up me and said he would shoot me if I didn't co-operate. My mother was there and she was beside herself pacing back and forth. My mother told my father that she would take the abuse to spare me. He took the rifle out of me and tried to get the other man to rape his own wife! (my mother).

He refused. He was married and he loved his wife; and he knew mom was my father's wife, and he knew it was wrong. It just kind of faded after that. Later, I heard that the man who hurt me so badly had died young and never got to have kids.

I remember the way dad looked at me when I tried to stop him from raping me. I have never seen such hatred and rage in my entire life. He said he would put the gun up my crotch, and this time he would shoot it. That terrible dark night I had a temper tantrum after it was all over. I told him I would cut off his penis if he ever tried anything like that again.

Until I was a sophomore in high school, we lived in a house that was among University of Maine fraternity buildings. I had the third floor, an attic, as my bedroom; we painted it chartreuse, my favorite color at the time. It was above the floor where my parents and sisters slept. It was quite convenient for my father. I was afraid each time I saw his head coming up the stairs. He performed those same sick sex acts on me that he and the other man had performed on me.

The rape ended after I got pregnant, but then my father demanded that I suck his penis and kiss his area until I was a freshman in high school. No more rape, but it was demanded of me that I service him in order to save my mother's life. He could very well have killed her.

One night he brought men home from Kiwanis. He invited his friends in to partake of my "services." He had bragged that he had a prostitute of his own, and they didn't believe him; so, he brought them with him to my private room on the third floor. I am pretty sure they had been drinking at the restaurant where the club members met. Somebody sang a dirty song. There was a scuffle, and I was screaming at the top of my lungs. They took my clothes off and held me down for others to rape me. They took off their pants and group raped me. I was screaming "Oh God, help me!" After a time, my mother and my younger sisters came upstairs with kitchen weapons. My mother said if they didn't leave, she would call the

35

cops. Somehow the sight of a woman they knew and her little kids with kitchen items brought them to their senses, and they sheepishly put their pants on and left. I was bleeding and badly hurt.

I had placed a mental grate in my mind in front of each man so as not to go mad because of the attack, and I still had my senses when they left. No one comforted me or helped me clean up afterwards, and it was never spoken of again.

For me it was traumatic. I believe that I still carry the trauma. It was a deep wound for my father to bring men home to rape me. It was bad enough that he used me on a regular basis, but to cheapen me further in that way was intolerable. Years later, God's Holy Spirit showed me the scene in a number of sessions because it was too troubling to see all at once. As I was processing the events mentally, God's Holy Spirit carried me to the beach and placed me in a beautiful gown and told me I was His beautiful child.

I had always thought my mother came up to save me from being raped. I would later find out that she wanted to ensure that none of the men would turn dad in. Her fear was that he would go to prison and there would be no money to care for the family.

Life carried on, and I lived it with no knowledge of the terrible things happening to me as I had dissociated from the terrible experiences. I had boyfriends, but we barely held hands. I think I played spin the bottle in someone's playroom; that was the extent of my foray into romantic relationships.

I had experiences away from home; but as I was always careful not to drink much alcohol, I kept myself safe. Keeping myself safe has always been a top priority with me wherever I have been. I grew up knowing I was responsible for my personal welfare, but I did not know why. When I read in a book years later that there were certain signs that indicated that a person had experienced trauma, I was stunned. The traumatized one was me! I remember thinking, "Run!" when there was no earthly reason for doing so.

God is good. He was ever with me although I didn't know it and didn't honor it. He was faithful, so faithful to me. I worked away from home summers. I couldn't wait to be far away from my parents. Mostly I worked as a waitress; I loved waitressing because I always loved to make people happy. I loved to work and thought I would work until I died. Later, I would realize that the Lord had other plans for me.

"the field"

Part Two: How God Healed Me

God had a plan for my life and found a way to direct me back to it by taking my job! My desperation sent me to Faith Worship Center where God began to restore my life and get me back to that wonderful plan.

1. Before Salvation

I have had a good life in many ways. I grew up as the eldest of five girls in a family with a father who could do anything and a mother who was a super mom. We lived in the second nicest home in town and had a big camp on a lake. My mother was church school superintendent and took us to the library every Saturday when we piled into the car with stacks of books. My dad donated a great deal of time to the Kiwanis Club and worked tirelessly for the good of his family and the good of the town. He maintained that huge camp because he wanted his girls to have access to the water, something he did not have as a boy growing up.

My dad had a problem, and it became my problem as well. He had a split personality, like Jekyll and Hyde; and the bad side was inhumanly cruel. He had been hurt by his father and split during a time of abuse. Unfortunately, no one understood what he was experiencing; so as far as I know, he never got help even if help had been available. My understanding is that helping a person with a split personality is close to impossible.

I've spent a great deal of time in ministry with the help of Jesus to uncover and heal all that occurred in my childhood. I know that I dissociated from a very young age (thankfully) so that I could go on with life. I also know that the memories started spilling out later and really demanded my attention.

I was brought up in a nice family and never lacked for food or drink or clothes or a bed or piano or violin or dance lessons or a college education. And I recognize that there is love in that; however, I looked out of the eyes of a child who did not know love. She did not believe she was even worthy of love. She hated herself and didn't even know it. I was loaded with anger and shame and self-loathing; but it was all underground, as I had dissociated and was stoic. I believed that if your own parents don't love you, you are unlovable. I know it is a lie, but I believe that most of the difficulties and losses I have faced stem from that core belief.

Fortunately, I was smart and fun-loving, so I didn't totally miss out on life. I had lots of friends, and I stayed away from home as much as possible. After graduating from college, I moved to Maryland for a good job and distance from my parents. I married, moved back to New England, and had two beautiful children and the beautiful life to go with it. I loved being a mother and working as a part-time project leader and computer programmer. Life was good. Then I divorced. Somehow divorce did not bring the life I had hoped for; rather, at that time I started realizing that I had had a tough childhood.

I learned about the abuse while taking a meditation course. My teacher was not a therapist, but she worked with me as memories surfaced. I came to believe that I had endured because I was strong and that my mind had saved me. I accepted that my father was a pedophile and struggled to go on with life.

Where was God? I believe that God was with me always in the person of Jesus, although I don't think I knew it until later. I wish I had known that He was with me! It would have been a great comfort.

I've spent many years gaining understanding and forgiving my parents, myself, and God and now am embarked on a different life—a life of ministry for survivors of incest and for incest perpetrators (many of whom were survivors of incest themselves).

I believe that sometime later, Jesus drew me to Him so that I could receive the healing I so desperately needed. First, He took my job! I told God that I was His, but that I couldn't do it myself. Three weeks later, I felt led to go to a swimming pool where I was a member. There I was ministered to and learned about Faith Worship Center, a believing church. Soon after, I began attending.

I became a born again Christian and gained deep love for the Lord. I received ministry for the brokenhearted under the guidance of the Holy Spirit. During ministry I learned that my father had a split personality with cruelty on the bad side and that his father had hurt him terribly in some of the same ways my father hurt me. I learned that Jesus was with me always and that it was because of Jesus that I was alive. I came to better understand the trials my parents faced and found forgiveness and love for them. Coming to wholeness was for me a process, not a onetime event, one that has allowed me to learn to believe that life is good and the world is a good place to be.

I remarried. Sometime later, in the midst of a snowstorm I had decided to shovel a foot of snow off my husband's car in order to show God I had forgiven my husband for something he had done. On the way back home, I heard in an audible voice: "a ministry for incest survivors." Those words have changed my life. They brought a meaning to my life I would never have expected. Under the guidance of the Holy Spirit, I pursued that ministry. Without God, I wouldn't have survived; and without God, I would not have had the privilege of ministry.

God has a plan for each person's life. Sometimes that plan gets derailed, and the person and the world are poorer for its loss. Often that plan gets derailed because Satan has found a way to block it, but sometimes we derail it ourselves by our behavior and choices. We live in a fallen world; yet God, our blessed Creator, is standing at the ready with a better way for us, a way to lead us back to the life that He intended for us. We each have purpose and a role to fulfill in life no matter how small it seems to us. If we don't fulfill our purpose in life, whatever we were to do doesn't get done. God can help us get back to that no matter how messed up our lives seem to be. Whatever the problem, the solution is always the same: GO TO GOD!

One of the ways God helped me before I really got to know Him was through dissociation. Have you ever spent time daydreaming, had highway hypnosis, or got lost in a book or movie? These are mild ways of losing touch with the awareness of your immediate surroundings. During trauma, dissociation is a way to help a person tolerate a situation that is too much to bear. God gave us the ability to dissociate so that life could continue until we could go to Him for help.

I started disassociating when I was a baby. I always knew there was "something wrong with me" or "something not quite right about me," and it wasn't until many years later that I learned I had disassociated and had many parts. (Having many parts indicates a condition called Dissociative Identity Disorder [DID], formerly known as Multiple Personality Disorder.) Dissociation was truly a blessing. I could not have moved forward in life if I had been aware always of the incredibly TERRIBLE things that happened to me. I created many parts, especially when I was a baby and a young child. Some of those parts did not look right when the Holy Spirit later showed them to me. I didn't know all this consciously until many years later when God started restoring my life. Little children don't usually know how to go to God for help, so they keep going as best they can.

Another way God helped me early in life was to take my spirit away to a beautiful place to rejuvenate me. This seems truly incredible, but it is true. Much later in life, my new friend who would one day become my husband led me up a long driveway on a hill and through the woods to a big field filled with tall grasses and black-eyed Susans. And, a magnificent view of Cold Stream Pond. When I finally arrived there as a much older adult, I cried and cried with the awareness of what God had done for me. My husband and I call this place "the field," and we occasionally visit to sense a strong connection with the Lord. It is truly heaven on earth. We have permission to be there, as we met the owner of the field. He said we could walk there any time.

On one of our visits to the field.

As a child I was very angry with God that He didn't come personally and take me out of the hell hole of a life I was living. I later learned that there was reason for me to be part of that life so I could tell the world of *the goodness of God.* We can't judge ourselves or others because only He TRULY knows what is occurring in our lives and why.

He also took my spirit out of the body when the abuse was more than I could handle. I know this because God's Holy Spirit showed this to me during sessions of ministry. It is remarkable how the Holy

Spirit can take a person back (in their mind and emotions) to a specific time in their life, and the person can then experience the event in the present to gain understanding and healing. What a person receives is an awareness and a knowing about an event. One of the times Holy Spirit took my spirit out of the body was when I was very small and my father got me from the bedroom and put me on the kitchen table to rape me. There is no need to carry old horrendous events in our being; in fact, we are vibrational and not designed to lug around a great deal of emotional baggage from the past. It hurts.

God was ALWAYS with me. I was never alone. I didn't know that when I was little, but I have seen that He was always there with me making things better. I know that Satan tried to get my mother to drown me when I was a baby with the belief that life would be better without me, and Jesus convinced her not to drown me. I have compassion for my mother who had a difficult role to play once she married my father and for my father, who had been truly burdened since childhood. Both are truly wonderful human beings now in heaven.

Another time God helped me was when my father burned down our neighborhood play house. With ministry I saw that Jesus stood with me as I watched it burn. And then as I lay on a bed in the room off the kitchen where my mother tended to my wounds, He tended to my spirit. He gave me the choice to live or die, and I chose to live. I always thought it was my mind that saved me, but it was Jesus who was always there in my darkest times. He is incredibly good to us even though we don't always know it.

As a child I had a problem, and I didn't know how to solve it. Back then I hadn't met the Creator, but I did believe there was a God. I thought He was a concept—as did the Greeks—and not a person. Now, although I have never seen Him, I believe He is a person, a rather incredible splendid person who watches over all of us and cares for each of us in ways I don't yet fathom. Would that I had known Him then; it would have saved me a great deal of grief, as I believed I had no one and no place to turn for help. I tried to help myself. I paced the beach and did a lot of child thinking there. How could I make things better?

I had heard that I was a pretty little girl, so I decided I would make myself ugly so my father would leave me alone. I screwed up my face and practiced looking ugly in the mirror; it didn't really help, and the belief I was ugly became a stronghold in my life. I thought of myself always as ugly, although others told me I was attractive. I believe that stronghold of my believing myself to be ugly interfered with my healing when I later had four surgeries on my nose after an automobile accident.

Much later, when I worked in the corporate world, I looked to New Age ideas for help. I thought New Age was God-focused; later I found that it wasn't. One of the avenues I followed was joining a group and meditating with their healing tapes. I attended a seminar in Portland, Oregon, with members from this group and was on my way to attend another. On the flight from Chicago to Portland, I sat next to a man named Pat Lynch. He told me that he had two years of training as a Jesuit, but had not taken vows. I told him about the seminar I was attending, about meditating with the group, about connecting with my soul, about sending illumined love to everyone. He asked me why I was connecting with my soul rather than praying to God—why I was part of a group rather than going straight to the source. I was rather startled. He asked me if I thought it was an accident we were seated together on the plane.

He took my emotional pain by praying over me and then recommended I not be part of the group, that I was a baby and a baby can be abused. He told me that God, not any sect, is the way to the Truth. He told me that what it is really about is that God is my Father and I am His child. I chose God over Guide Jaiwa and Launa Huffines, the founder of the school (the School of Illumination). Pat then paid for me to stay in the Marriott Hotel in Portland, arranged for me to call his mother and see a priest, and gave me cab money! I was shocked to the core. Stunned.

I had then had a vision that I was at the razor's edge about to commit my life to teaching a set of tapes that were from the wrong side. I was in a room with broken mirrors on the floor, symbolic of false prophets.

I owe a great deal to the Lord and Pat Lynch. I had been asking God to help me since I was a child, but evidently not really willing or able to receive it. The night before I met Pat Lynch, I had told myself in a time of quiet that I was not going to live like this anymore and that I was no longer going to be used by anyone. GOD IS SO GOOD!!!

I don't really know God's plan for healing me. I can only write about what I've been through, but I know God well enough to know that He was always there, guiding me and others to provide for my healing.

My Mother prayed for help for me for years. God bless her! Her insistent prayers for me to get to God finally bore fruit when Jesus took my job away from me. I was really angry when I realized that He arranged that, but I finally accepted that He wanted me to heal from the pain I was carrying. I, of course, was afraid. I loved to work, and I thought it was my mind that had kept me alive and managing life as best I could. Although I had stock in the stock market and some savings, I didn't know how I would manage financially without a job, and I needed a job to keep my mind happy.

I became DESPERATE. I went into my bedroom and reached out to God and told Him I was His, but I couldn't do it alone. Three weeks later I sensed that I should head to the indoor pool where I was a member. I met Steve Cummings who attended Faith Worship Center in Pepperell, Massachusetts. He found me swimming and crying in the lane next to his, and we talked. I told him that I had known for a while that I wanted to be a healer, and he told me there was a church with a focus on healing and how to contact it. Then, he and his son prayed over me. I contacted that church and started attending weekly.

Through God's love and caring, little by little, He put me back together. It was not easy, but it was possible. If He did that for me who was so terribly afflicted, He will do that for you if you turn to Him. It is His **grace,** His unmerited favor, that forgives you and provides a companion, His Holy Spirit, to guide you. NO SIN IS TOO BIG FOR GOD!!! Go to God and talk with Him, for He loves you and will help you set your life to rights. It will take time.

2. Salvation

Psalm 23

A Psalm of David

1 The LORD is my shepherd; I shall not want.

2 He maketh me to lie down in green pastures: he leadeth me beside the still waters.

3 He restoreth my soul: he leadeth me in the paths of righteousness for His name's sake.

4 Yea, though I walk through the valley of the shadow of death, I will fear no evil: for thou *art* with me; thy rod and thy staff they comfort me.

5 Thou preparest a table before me in the presence of mine enemies: thou anointest my head with oil; my cup runneth over.

6 Surely goodness and mercy shall follow me all the days of my life: and I will dwell in the house of the LORD for ever. (KJV)

I had been abused in every way possible. I had learned of the abuse earlier and had spent enormous energy and time and money getting help for myself, but I was in no way following God's plan for my life. By the time I got to Faith Worship Center (FWC), I was in my early sixties, depressed and feeling unworthy; and I had just lost my job. I believed that I was unlovable and ugly and that my needs didn't matter, although those were mostly unconscious beliefs. My two adult children were happily married and doing well. I was married to my second husband and living with him and two Maine Coon cats in a townhouse community in an upstanding town. Little did I know that God had a plan to restore my soul and direct me back to that wonderful plan He had intended for me. I would meet God's Holy Spirit, and He would be my guide along a unique path that would lead to my restoration and to His plan for my life.

Meeting Jesus and Holy Spirit changed my life. There was this whole area of life about which I knew nothing. At Faith Worship Center I was saved by the grace of God through the gift of faith[2]. Pastor Daryl Nicolet prayed a prayer of salvation with me and I accepted Jesus as my Lord and Savior. I experienced a spiritual rebirth becoming born again (born from above). This spiritual rebirth produced spiritual life in me: I was now alive spiritually[3] with an ever-present relationship with God!

I had God's life in me. I was born of God. I was now God's child and part of His family of children with brothers and sisters in Christ. I had a new identity of "much-loved child of God following Jesus." This was a much better identity than incest survivor, and I told myself repeatedly that I was a much-loved child of God following Jesus to break the old idea of being a victim.

Around this time, God provided His Holy Spirit as a companion for me to teach, guide, and comfort me along the path of much change to come. I was now beaming with God's very life, Spirit, and nature. I was now saved and destined for heaven with the eternal life

---

[2] Ephesians 2:8-10 "For it is by grace you have been saved, through faith—and this not from yourselves, it is the gift of God—not by works, so that no one can boast. For we are God's workmanship, created in Christ Jesus to do good works, which God prepared in advance for us to do." (NIV)

[3] John 10:10 "…I have come that they may have life and have it to the full." (NIV)

of Christ abiding within me. Hallelujah! I had no idea at the time of how wonderful it could be to live in the light with the Lord.

It took some time for me to begin to realize what had just happened to me. I was now a child of God and not a child of Satan. It was an incredible shock to me to realize sometime later that I had been part of Satan's kingdom and not God's Kingdom. I had always considered myself a good person who loved people and did what I thought was right. I had taught Sunday School as a young person for my mother who was church school superintendent at my home town church. I had gone to church consistently other than during college. With this new way of following Jesus, I had to re-examine my world view. I read a wonderful book called *God at War: The Bible and Spiritual Conflict* by Gregory A. Boyd that helped tremendously even though there was much that was beyond my understanding at the time. The Holy Spirit had begun a process of re-creating and transforming me from the old life to the new life. I was now a completely new creation.

And I was about to begin a process of inner healing. When I got saved, my spiritual heart needed some attention because of all the trials I had experienced and choices I had made. Inner healing is a process by which a person heals (is no longer impacted) from the consequences of dealing with the hurts of life. I found that I had attitudes and strongholds (stuck places in my mind) that had affected areas of my spiritual heart.

I learned that I hated my mother. My son had a punching bag I had pounded hundreds of times with his gloves and spoken the words, "Mothers are supposed to love their children." I thought I was past all of that, but I needed to say it—express it. I was shocked first upon realizing that I hated her and second that I didn't know about it. I certainly didn't act as if I hated her. Surely, I loved her!

Little by little, Holy Spirit brought healing opportunities to me, and I welcomed them with open arms. One day during worship at FWC, something deep inside me broke, and I started sobbing. A friend came and held me. The worship singing continued as long as my healing needed to continue! Another time while talking with a friend, deep shame came to the surface. My friend held me for what seemed like hours as layer after layer of shame emerged and left me for good. A third time, a professor held me after a deep group exercise in a course on spirituality.

I read everything I could find about healing, books like *Open My Heart Lord: Healing For The Brokenhearted* by Kathi Oates with Robert Paul Lamb, *Help For The Fractured Soul: Experiencing Healing and Deliverance from Deep Trauma* by Candyce Roberts, and *The Effects of Trauma: And How to Deal With It* by Jim Banks, among many others.

Faith Worship Center has a room set aside for prayer where faith-based music plays twenty-four hours a day. The Presence of the Holy Spirit can be felt strongly there at times, and the prayer room is a place where deep healing can occur. There is nothing like experiencing the Presence of the Lord!

Often other Christians are there in the prayer room for support and hands-on healing. I received much inner healing by spending time in the prayer room and by attending Faith Worship Center's church services. FWC is a non-denominational church that believes in the Bible and is in many ways a center for transformation. Its website, www.faithworship.org, states its vision as, "To live as a people who establish the will of God and the power of His kingdom here on earth as it is in heaven." (Accessed April 25, 2022.) Attending the Sunday morning service gave me a much-needed personal reboot especially during times of much change and healing from the past. I attended classes at Faith Worship Center on how to heal, how to pray, and how to prophecy. I also attended many outside speaker events held at Faith Worship Center on weekends. I had the privilege of attending church there for many years. Daryl and Lyn Nicolet are extraordinary Christians who lovingly minister God's grace and love. I grew up in the faith there and consider it my church away from home, my forever church.

I also spent almost ten years in a home group associated with Faith Worship Center. A home group is a fairly small group of generally church attendees that get together. I had never met such wonderful people. We usually met once a week to fellowship, share testimonies, and learn together. Jonathan and Cindy Gale and Paul and Leslie Gosselin led our group. I felt mentored and incredibly privileged! As a new Christian, I peppered the group with questions. It was so good to have someone to ask! As Jonathan told me that first Sunday at Faith Worship Center, it can be a long time between Sunday mornings.

Faith Worship Center welcomed many wonderful speakers from other ministries. Many of those speakers profoundly impacted my life. One of them was Kathi Oates who led me to the healing I was seeking. Kathi ministered healing to a packed audience at church, and I was deeply touched. I held myself together emotionally so those on either side of me would not be impacted by the intense inner experience I was having, but the healing was deep. I learned from Kathi that it was Andy Miller who had worked with her and her husband, Gary Oates, and she recommended him highly.

Andy Miller is a therapist and spirit-filled Christian who has an incredible healing ministry and has helped a great many people hurt in the way I was hurt and other ways as well. I searched for him after Gary and Kathi Oates ministered at Faith Worship Center. Finding and working with Andy Miller gave me real hope for my life.

When Andy helped me realize that I had dissociated from a young age, I was quite upset. I didn't know that was what it was called. I soon came to be grateful that God had provided a way for me to put aside experiences that were too much to process at the time they happened. Andy Miller helped me process the experiences that had caused me to split into many dissociated parts. We worked over the phone in many sessions. Andy guided our sessions with the Holy Spirit who brought to mind past experiences in incredible detail so that I was right there mentally and emotionally with the experience. Andy helped me process each experience that came to light. With God's help, I went through a process of forgiving and blessing the person(s) who had hurt me.

Part of Andy's healing work is to bring the dissociated part or parts back into the person with the overall goal of becoming a whole human being. I spent about eleven months working with Andy once a week, and after that, as needed. I received about an hour's healing with each telephone session. Between sessions, I processed what we had learned. The work was not always easy, but it was always a time of deep inner healing. Andy is now Father Andrew Miller, LCSW, and the founder and president of HeartSync Ministries (https://www.heartsyncministries.org/about/) [4].

I also received Sozo ministry at Faith Worship Center. Sozo, a term found in the Bible, means saved, healed, and delivered. Christian ministry teams have developed Sozo ministry into a lay healing ministry under the guidance of the Holy Spirit. Two lay persons prayerfully work together in a session under the guidance of the Holy Spirit in a church setting. They offer it to church members and non-church members for a small fee. In a two-hour session, a person who is struggling in life can gain inner healing and answers to life's troubling questions. Nancy Duprey and Connie Messer administered Sozo to me in many sessions. The Sozo team now give a Sozo participant time to process between sessions, but I had many sessions back-to-back. I also learned to administer Sozo for others as part of the team. It is an incredible privilege to be able to administer healing through God's Holy Spirit. Often, I saw years of pain and struggle leave a person's face after two hours of receiving this ministry. A church that offers Sozo ministry will list it on its website. Bethel Church in California is in many ways a mother church in this area. Detailed information about Sozo can be found

---

[4] "He has practiced as a professional individual, marriage and family therapist since 1990. The bulk of his practice is focused on resolving severe desynchronization (scriptural brokenheartedness) in those suffering from abuse and trauma. He actively incorporates biblical healing principles with sound clinical practice." (Accessed April 19, 2022.)

on its website. Books are also available that teach about this ministry. The book *Sozo for Professional Counselors: Integrating Psychology and Inner Healing to Restore Individuals to Wholeness* by Margaret Nagib, Psy.D., is also available for mental health professionals.

I would never go back to the old ways. I had depression—lots of it. Now I have joy—His joy! Would I swap His joy for my depression? Certainly not. I am a happy person full of gratitude for what the Lord has done for me and in my life. I rarely think about the past except to think about how I can help those hurt as I was. There are many of us. My graduate school advisor at Andover Newton Theological School (now Andover Newton Seminary at Yale Divinity School) suggested that I tailor each class to what I could learn for my ministry, and I did. I wrote a fifty-page paper as my last assignment, and I learned that experts believe that maybe twenty percent of girls and five percent of boys have the experience of incest. That is horrendous. Why is there no outrage, no outcry? I believe it is because incest has such a taboo associated with it, and it is underreported and underdiscussed. No one wants to say they were hurt in that way.

The only way I know to heal that terrible hurt is to talk about it and to get healing for what happens to a person when someone crosses their personal boundary. Children love their parents no matter how inappropriate they are with them, and the child comes to believe it is her or his fault. It can take years to unravel the wrong ideas and troubles that come to a person who had incest as a companion to their childhood (and sometimes beyond childhood).

A friend gave me the book *The Prince of Tides* by Pat Conroy when I was recuperating from a serious automobile accident that flattened my nose. The book tells of a sexual attack on a family by two men from prison. The family's pet tiger killed the men, and the family buried them. No one spoke of what had happened; each carried the trauma in their own way to their personal detriment. We are vibrational beings, and we are not designed to carry trauma for years. We need to process it, express it, and give it to God.

It took years of therapy and ministry and counseling to get me to the happy place I now live. I have spent years and years of my life getting past all that occurred in my childhood. I might have been truly living life during that time. I am not complaining, but I think of all the lives that have been impacted by this thing called incest. So many never get to a happy place, and that is a tragedy. Survivors take on beliefs about themselves that are not positive and then live out of that belief system until someone or something comes to break the unhappy patterns.

I have my own beliefs about what is under incest. I believe Satan uses incest to keep a very large portion of the population away from that wonderful life God promises.

3. My God is Real

There are many of us—adults who have grown up with traumatic childhoods. The human body is not designed to carry so much unacknowledged trauma, so it develops afflictions of many kinds. Did you know that emotions can "hang out" in the lungs or elsewhere if they aren't expressed? I stuffed my emotions as a child and had frozen emotions until I started really dealing with what had happened to me. It was not safe for me to feel what I felt: I might have said something that could have gotten me killed.

As a child I found my way to the corner service station where there were Sugar Daddies for sale. I had little sweetness in my life, so sugar seemed to help, and so I began my lifelong adventure in dental chairs. As a teen I took iron pills because I had no energy, and I coughed a lot. In college, I drank gallons of coffee to keep going. I mean gallons! And cigarettes too. I had no clue that deep down I had a dark secret from my childhood. It has taken many years to unravel all that happened to me, how the trauma manifested, and what to do with it.

I have learned how important it is to express my feelings. Emotions don't always tell the truth; but whether truthful or not, they have an impact on the body if they are not expressed. I try not to stuff my feelings now, but sometimes I still do unconsciously. It is better for me to acknowledge my feelings and take some kind of action when they happen or soon after.

I would like to think that most people learn how to deal with their feelings as they grow up. I didn't, and I am still having to learn how best to deal with them. Depression can be an unwelcome result of not facing feelings head on. I believe that I am mostly past having constant hurt feelings from rejection, but it has been a real trial learning how. Once I acknowledge a hurt feeling and try to understand what in me allowed that, I try to remember to give it to God.

Believe me, some of these unexpressed emotions are raw and really painful. I don't want them to hang out with me forever, and they can if I don't notice them. I choose to forgive others and ask God to bless them in order to set things to rights. It works and keeps me happy and laughing, a way I want to be.

Once I started getting help, I learned what my feelings were as a child: *it hurt to be me.* I was terribly afraid because I never knew when I would be hurt next; getting hurt seemed to come out of the blue. It was not possible to protect myself. Crying didn't help; screaming didn't help. I hated my life. No one outside the family knew what was happening inside my family, and my parents were well regarded in the community. I didn't like being their child. I was terrified of my father. He had all the power in the family. He had the guns and made all the money. What he said went. Even my mother had fear of my father. She did what she could to keep him from drinking too much because you never knew what he would do when he had too much to drink.

I remember the way my father looked at me—the rage in his eyes—like little spots of red directed at me. I didn't like it. My cat Mittens was the only thing in all the world that loved me, and my dad ran over him one Thanksgiving. After that, I had no love at all.

I felt so alone: God had forsaken me and put me on this planet with two monsters that hadn't the first idea how to love and care for a child. I felt totally cut off from nourishment of any kind. My next younger sister tried to take care of me as best she could. God bless her! I was filled with shame and pain. I ran to my mother about being so badly hurt, and she did not help me. I felt deserted by God.

I lived in terror of my father. I was so afraid he would hurt me. His body smelled of vegetable soup (an unclean unwashed smell), alcohol, and stale cigarette smoke. I dreaded that smell; I smelled it up close, and I didn't like it. I learned that I had used my mind to keep me sane when he was torturing me. In my mind I cut his body into little squares. It was the only defense I had.

Later, when I became a Christian, I had to repent and ask God for forgiveness for wanting to murder my father. (It seemed perfectly natural to me at the time to want to kill him when he was hurting me so badly.) For many years, I had the seemingly illogical worry that I would murder my father; some part of me must have known what had transpired in my early years. At times when he was hurting me, I saw rage in his eyes that had nothing to do with me. I was terrified of his anger. He was incredibly mean. He had a kind side, but he was MEAN. And he was stern. Nobody dared look at him crosswise. I loved my father, and I hated my father.

I felt the sadness from the womb! about not being wanted by my mother. I believed I was unlovable because my own mother tried to abort me and didn't love me. I did everything in my power to get my parents to love me, and yet my mother hated me and my father raped and terrorized me. I felt totally unloved and all alone in the world. If your own parents don't love you, who will? I came to believe that no matter what I did, no one would ever love me. I steeled myself to that reality and accepted it for many years.

It was not fun to feel those feelings! Session after session, Andy and I released trauma after trauma and the trapped feelings that were under those memories. I cried buckets. And little by little, I got better and happier.

I also learned how it felt to be an adult. I still don't always know how I feel despite practicing knowing how I feel. I was crying on the inside about being repeatedly raped. I was a child and was raped and nobody helped me. Nobody ever talked about it. We just acted as if it didn't happen. I had a deep sense of injustice about what happened in my childhood that manifested as primal rage trapped in my body.

I never had a chance to be a little girl; I was robbed of my childhood and lost my innocence too young. I suffered from my father's designation of me as a prostitute. I WAS NOT A PROSTITUTE. I was angry that my mother assumed that I would always take care of her. My shoulders carried false burdens. My father said that if I was not available to him, he would murder the whole family. And he would have.

I experienced a few "side effects" from my childhood. I believed I was ugly, unlovable, unworthy, and that my needs didn't matter. I existed only to make things better for others. My need to be safe was a stronghold that kept courage at bay. I felt as if I were peering out from the bushes when I went out to be sure I would be okay. I had incredible fear, anger, panic attacks, depressions, psoriasis, and experienced painful rejection that kept me in emotional turmoil much of the time.

I became a born again Christian in 2005. In early 2014 I learned that Father God was taking down the barriers I had erected to protect myself from the world. In April of that year, I saw the movie *The Horse Whisperer* and realized that like the horse whisperer, Jesus had been gentling me for a long time to be willing to believe that I wouldn't be hurt if I let go of my protective walls. I told Him I wanted a real life. I had been terribly afraid to be my real self for fear of being vulnerable and hurt.

I was afraid for many years although I didn't really know it! Looking back, I can see how much that fear dominated my life and my choices. I was in the car the first time I had a panic attack, so I stopped at the library. There I found a book that told me what I had and to practice deep breathing to counteract it. I also told myself that I wasn't going to allow myself to panic, that there was nothing pressing. It helped.

Once I began inner healing, I started repeating several scriptures - the 23ʳᵈ Psalm and Isaiah 41:10 - which Jonathan Gale gave me on my first day at FWC:

Isaiah 41:10

Do not fear, for I am with you;

Do not anxiously look about you, for I am your God.

I will strengthen you, surely I will help you,

Surely I will uphold you with my righteous right hand. (NASB)

Repeating those scriptures helped. I used to say, "Fear, go!", and usually it would go. In truth there is fear or love; once I became a closer follower of the Lord, fear just sort of dropped out of my life. Hallelujah!

Dealing with anger has been a life lesson for me. I had a lot to be angry about. And I was angry, very angry. I used my son's boxing gloves and punching bag over and over to deal with how I felt about my mother giving me to my father and not protecting me. I worked with therapists and followed their suggestions. I read books on how to deal with anger. I took it out on myself in the form of depression; I didn't want to hurt others with my anger.

Years later, I realized that often the anger came when I felt unloved by people who I thought were supposed to love me. *Will no one ever love me?* I give and give and give and no one gives back. I know it is not true, but it can *feel* true. If my own parents couldn't love me, who would? I finally decided to honor the truth of Psalm 37:8, "Cease from anger, and forsake wrath; Do not fret—it only causes harm" (NKJV) and to choose love over anger. At Holy Spirit's suggestion, I repent every day for using anger as a way to cope with life. There are better ways, like remembering to be thankful for all the good things. That is where I want my focus to be.

I had one major depression and many minor ones. I never took antidepressants because I wanted to stay myself and was concerned that I would never be able to get off the medication. I studied depression in books and in a master's level course. I learned that some people had it much worse than I had. The closer I got to the Lord the easier it became to not allow depression into my life. I found a little handbook by Joyce Meyer called *Straight Talk on Depression: Overcoming Emotional Battles with the Power of God's Word!* The truth in that little book set me free, and I have had no more depression. Praise the Lord! Hallelujah!

Have you ever been triggered emotionally back to another time by something that happens in the present? Usually, the present event is nowhere near as painful emotionally as the past event. I used to experience rejection constantly, and it triggered me back to feelings I had as a child when my mother gave me to my father to use while she loved on my baby sister. These were feelings of rage, jealousy, and the one not chosen. I was constantly bathed in those horrible feelings and didn't know why. I just knew I felt regularly rejected. It didn't take much to trigger me, so I lived often in that awful time.

Through ministry I learned I had been living in a vortex of rejection, another reality similar to the Matrix! Jesus had told me He was leading me out of the shadows, and I realized He was leading me out of this other reality. What a revelation for someone who had had countless tribulations.

Several years later, I continued to work through issues of rejection that were not as deep and was able to make some much-needed change: I would keep my heart centered on Jesus rather than on the person who seemed to be rejecting me. I would realize it wasn't really about me at all. I would "brush" or "shake off" the unwanted feelings. I would remind myself of the words from Acts 20:24, "But none of these things move me..." (KJV). I would learn to rejoice in all circumstances. It worked! Now that feelings of rejection are no longer haunting me, I can enjoy life, and that is something God wants for each one of us. Eureka!!

4. What is Sexual Addiction?

During one ministry session, I asked Andy how a grown man could find a two-year-old attractive for sex. He told me that he had been listening to Jim Wilder[5] tapes on sexual addiction. Evidently men who molest can have severe attachment issues. I had learned in another setting that my dad had been severely molested and hurt by his own father and that the horrible things he did to me had been done to him by his own dad. Evidently men (or women) who molest can long for attachment (emotional closeness) and can become addicted to sex desperately seeking intimacy. Once such a person acts out their need sexually, it becomes difficult to stop. My understanding is that acting out sexually turns off the lack of attachment switch in the brain, and the person then wrongly assumes that s/he feels better until the good feelings wear off. Andy helped me see that my father was a sex addict with a perverse spirit on the bad side. I now know that his sexual addiction was born out of the difficulties from his own childhood.

In December of 2014, I earned a Master of Arts in Theological Studies at Andover Newton Theological School. My focus was pastoral ministry, concentrating on helping survivors of incest. Holy Spirit had nudged me to look into graduate school five or so years earlier, and I had jumped at the chance—I love school! I believe

---

[5] Dr. Jim Wilder (Ph.D. Clinical Psychology and M.A. Theology Fuller Theological Seminary) author of *The Life Model: Living from the Heart Jesus Gave You.*

attending theology school was another way God healed me. You cannot work your way through theology courses without undergoing much inner change!

Our ceremony was May 2015.

I took a course in Idolatry or Illness: Pastoral Care and Counseling with Addictions. For that course I presented to the class on the guiding question "What is Sexual Addiction?" I found that my father was far from alone in having to cope with behavior formerly coined "hyper sexual disorder," the former name for sex addiction. Although the disorder was not included as an official psychiatric disorder in the DSM-5 (Diagnostic and Statistical Manual of Mental Disorders, 5th Edition: published by the American Psychiatric Association), that kind of behavior has ruined lives and brought disastrous consequences for many. Doing the research gave me a real look at the disorder and a level of understanding and compassion for anyone—including my father—who suffered with the illness.

In 1983, Dr. Patrick J. Carnes, Ph.D., now an internationally known authority and speaker on sex addiction and recovery issues, authored the first clinical book on the condition based on his own research, *Out of the Shadows: Understanding Sexual Addiction.* Now in its third edition the book provides an in-depth look at the disorder and guides the reader out of the shadows and into a better life. He includes a detailed Resource Guide and directs the reader to www.sexhelp.com for the latest on what is available to help sex addicts. His own website www.drpatrickcarnes.com provides tests for the viewer to assist in answering the question "Am I a Sex Addict?" It tells the viewer that if the answer is yes, to start therapy with a Certified Sex Addiction Therapist and to join a 12-step program for sex addiction.

With others, Carnes compiled material about sex addiction from almost one thousand sex addicts who filled out detailed personal surveys and participated in interviews. They told their life stories willingly in order to help bring understanding to a very dark place with which they were familiar. They told about self-destructive sexual behavior they were not able to stop, and they defined recovery as "transformation from a life of self-destruction to a life of self-care."[6]

Ted Roberts is a former fighter pilot in Vietnam who is now a pastor and author. His book *Pure Desire: How One Man's Triumph Can Help Others Break Free From Sexual Temptation* speaks to his experience with sexual addiction and others he helped break free from sexual difficulties. He notes that the great majority of men he counseled

---

[6] Patrick J. Carnes, Ph.D., *Don't Call It Love: Recovery From Sexual Addiction* (New York: Bantam Books, 1991), 1-2.

who had sex addiction had "father wounds in their souls."[7]

It appears that a great deal of help is available for someone who recognizes that help is needed. There are a number of treatment centers, residential facilities, hospitals, treatment fellowship groups, therapists, and 12-step programs available. The Meadows in Wickenburg, Arizona, appears to be a premier treatment program. Its site states,

> Sex addiction, also known as sexual compulsivity or sexual dependency, is defined as a pathological relationship with a mood-altering experience. In short, it's compulsive behavior—of a sexual nature in this case—that diminishes someone's life. Those struggling with sexual addiction will prioritize sex above everything else, even family, friends, and work. Given how sex becomes the organizing principle, the person struggling is willing to sacrifice other things they care about in pursuit of unhealthy behavior. At The Meadows, we are able to address these issues during treatment…[8]

---

[7] Ted Roberts, *Pure Desire: How One Man's Triumph Can Help Others Break Free From Sexual Temptation* (Ventura, CA: Regal, 1999), 65.

[8] www.themeadows.com/addiction-treatment/sex-addiction/(accessed August 7, 2021).

5. Life is Good!

Healing is most definitely a process; and as long as we are willing, it will go forward. Over the years, I unknowingly "adopted" many mothers to fill a deeply felt need. With ministry I came to truly love my own mother and realize that she and dad and I had come for a mission to help others. I visited her many times in her older years. One time, she kissed my hands over and over. She had never done that before. She told me "ONWARD," which I believe meant go do your thing (ministry for incest survivors to which I had been called and of which she knew). On the way driving home, I realized I had been overjoyed to see her.

For me, it was an acknowledgment that she realized the three of us had come for a mission to help incest survivors and to get out the word about the goodness of God as part of our life plans. I cried buckets. It was extremely tough on each one of us, but worth it if some good came out of it. Much healing came from this time with my dear mom.

I had the incredibly good fortune to be part of a group of Christian women called CRAVE and to attend two years of Faith School of Supernatural Ministry (FSSM) taught by Faith Worship Center. I learned a great deal and, in the process, attained additional spiritual maturity. I decided to stop stuffing my feelings and be accountable for them and to be willing to care for myself and let love in in a new way. I also repented from allowing anyone to use me for my survival because I am a daughter of the King (Jesus). I came to the end of myself and felt His life in me! for the first time. How sweet it is!!! I decided to look up and as much as possible out of His eyes. Holy Spirit provided all of this because He loves me so much!

Holy Spirit had asked me a year earlier if I would like to go to Iona. Would I ever! Iona is an island in the Inner Hebrides off the west coast of Scotland; it is considered a "thin place" close to heaven and a desirable place to visit. I signed up to spend a week there with a group of dispersed Christians dedicated to peace and justice. On our last evening there, we submitted prayer requests that were prayed over and sent to heaven. That night in bed, I was able to accept my sexuality. That was no small matter after all that I had been through. The next morning, I spoke of it at my breakfast table and then headed to my room in a hurry where I sobbed for twenty minutes. I was heard and not judged. Praise God!

Years earlier, I had heard that infants in some foreign land had missing brain cells because they had been raised in an orphanage without love. Something about that story clicked with me. I had spent my life loving others with no expectation of return and not really knowing that that was not normal. According to Holy Spirit, there were times Jesus lavished affection over me, and I had no awareness of it. I had such a love deficit over all my years on planet earth that I didn't even recognize when I was being loved. I had given and given and gotten little in return.

July 5, 2017, Holy Spirit set up a divine appointment with a Christian named George Stevens who had lost his wife of many years to cancer. We met at Cold Stream Pond near the place Holy Spirit had taken my spirit to give me courage to go on. As we got to know each other, Holy Spirit worked with each of us. He told me, "The path of true love has ups and downs. When you get to truly know each other, quirks and foibles will seem less surprising." I took that to heart.

Although I had been married twice before, I truly had no inner framework for being loved by a man. During our getting to know each other, I also had to acknowledge that there is give and take in relationships not just give. I had to learn to receive from another. One time he was especially kind to me, and an iron wall that I had built to protect myself came off my spiritual heart. I sobbed and sobbed from not being loved as a child. That wall had protected me from those feelings for many years. All it took was a little kindness from a loved one to bring great healing! He comforted me and held me for hours. Love is an incredible gift that we can give to each other.

Part Three: The Goodness of God

It is impossible to overstate the goodness of God. He is WITH us. He is FOR us. He LOVES us.

1. Fundamentals

Envision a beautiful banner in the sky that says,
"Go to God for He loves you dearly."

I didn't always know it at the time, but my God was always with me. He never left my side. When the abuse was too much for me, He took me out of the body. I endured, but He endured with me. All those years of terrible suffering are long past now, but I grieve for children who are currently enduring incest, child pornography, trafficking, molestation, and rape. There is NO NEED for any of that in God's world; and I believe there will be a time when suffering will cease, and the world will be as God intended.

I have the incredibly good fortune to be a child of God now, and He is present with me always. It is a magnificent way to live—with the guidance of the Holy Spirit. God takes care of those who turn to Him. That is all that is needed, to repent and turn from the old ways and embrace the goodness of God. He made you; He knows your every breath, your every thought, and your every move. He truly knows what you need long before you do. He kisses your face with His sweet kisses and sings to you when you are asleep. He looks way ahead and sets things up for you in line with your highest best good. You have a calling on your life, and He will show you the steps to take to find it and act on it. Here is a prayer you can pray right now. Holy Spirit gave it to me so that I could pray it with my father:

> Prayer for Salvation:
>
> I believe Jesus is the Son of God
>
> He died on the cross to take our sin
>
> I believe He is alive today
>
> I am sorry for my sin and ask you to forgive me
>
> I receive Jesus as my Lord and Savior
>
> I believe I am saved and will spend eternity with You.

You can now give over any sin to Him. Bundle it up and hand it to the Lord Jesus Christ.

You will need the companionship of other Christians as you become more like Him. They have already been through what you are going through and can help you along the way. Find a church that believes the Bible is true and attend every Sunday. Listen for that still small voice of the Holy Spirit who will love you and guide you and help you become more like Jesus.

Jesus is such a blessing to me! If I really need His Presence to come in a fuller way, all I need to do is turn on some worship music and sing with it. It makes me incredibly happy to worship because somehow, He comes; and I sense His Presence. It is His Presence, His love, His caring, the life that is possible when you know Him that makes life worthwhile. He brings life. Yes, you are alive, but if you don't know Jesus, you are really living dead (spiritually).

It is so different to be alive with the Lord. You are walking that narrow path that leads to eternal life with God. There is so much joy in being alive with Him. It is more than the regular joy some people have and that is wonderful; it is His joy which can't be suppressed and bubbles out from you. Life's little troubles look different when you have the love of the Lord and His joy bubbling out from you. Little things bring joy—the song of a bird, the sensation of water on your face, the smile of another human being. So much falls by the wayside when He is your companion in life.

He is asking me to tell you about wonder. When you were a little child, did you not find the world a wonderful place? Did you not wonder who held up the stars or how chocolate ice cream got made? Did you wonder about four-leaf clovers and where could you find one? Do you ever wonder now? How you came about? What was God thinking when He made you? What are you supposed to be doing with your time and your life?

God cares so very much about each one of us. He wants us to acknowledge Him, the Creator of all things. We did not create ourselves. We were not made in a vacuum. Each of us has an important role to play in life, and when we don't take on our assigned role, it does not get done. Something is missing when you fail to step up and be who God made you to be. Part of that calling we each have is to understand that we are part of His creation, and each one of us is responsible for acknowledging our Creator and thanking Him for all He has done for us. He is a good God, and He is to be honored and worshipped by each of us.

God exists in a Trinity: God the Father, God the Son (Jesus), and God the Holy Spirit. It seemed an awkward arrangement when I first heard of it, but it works well. Father God is a spiritual being who lives in heaven—and He is a person. We look like Him! Jesus is His son, the Creator of the world, and the part of God that came to earth to save us. His Presence can be felt by individual believers. I have no idea how this works, but it is a tremendous comfort in times of trouble.

The Holy Spirit can be both inside you and on you. This concept can be hard to understand, but it is true. We who are believers are considered to be the temple of the Holy Spirit; in other words, God's spirit dwells inside us and gives us direction. There are times when the power of the Holy Spirit comes to reside upon a believer. This happens, for example, when healing has been requested, and the Holy Spirit comes to provide it. God is so much more than I can describe; I CAN say that a lifetime of learning about Him and loving Him brings great rewards to a believer.

I always believed in God, but I thought He was a concept! No, He is a being, an extraordinary being who defies anything a human can define. I was in my sixties when I met Him. Don't wait! Get to know Him as soon as possible! Your life will never be the same. You will find such love as you've never known. St. Augustine wrote of that hole in the heart of every human that can only be filled by the love of God. Nothing else can match God's love, and a person who finds God generally won't turn back, because there is nothing else in life that satisfies that longing as the love of the Lord.

There is so much I can tell you about the life of the believer. It is not like that of the unbeliever, because the believer does their best to keep their eyes on Jesus. My best way to live is "eyes on Jesus/ one day at a time/ following the Holy Spirit." I don't really see Jesus on a daily basis; there is no form in my mind's eye. It is a mindset I have adopted which keeps my focus on what He would want of me. Focus is critical. It directs your life. With my focus on the Lord, I am screening out much of life that is meaningless and does not bring life. I believe that some actually "see" a form. I have "seen" Him a few times, but I don't "see" Him on a regular basis.

"One day at a time" reminds me not to dwell on the past or worry about the future. Today is enough to consider for today. I do plan ahead, but don't travel about my day thinking much about the future. "Following the Holy Spirit" means that as much as possible, I choose to allow God's Holy Spirit to direct my steps. It can take a little time to adopt this way of living, but it is certainly preferable to how I used to live. This way of living has become a happy habit.

I don't look different from others, but I am aware that I am different. I'm in God's army, as in "Onward Christian Soldiers." I am a revolutionary in the best meaning of the word. Spiritual warfare (praying against the dark side) is a crucial part of being a Christian and a protection against the activities of evil. Planet earth belongs to Satan and his minions. You may not be able to accept that. The evil that exists in the world was put there by Satan's associates and drives much of what goes on in the world. It took me some time to really get what is happening on this planet; but once I did, I understood why things seem so crazy and, in many ways, so wrong. I have learned to pray against his activity in my life and in the lives of my loved ones by pleading the blood of Jesus in my prayers and by being observant and ever aware.

God's Word, the Bible, has become important to me. Many new believers study the Bible and find wisdom and guidance there. I tried but found it hard to understand until my husband George gave me a Bible heavily footnoted. What a blessing it has been to read the Word of God with a tutor in the footnotes. There are Psalms to read to soothe the soul and comfort you when emotions are running amuck. I particularly love Psalm 27 because of verse 13 which says:

I would have lost heart, unless I had believed

That I would see the goodness of the LORD in the land of the living. (NKJV)

It brings me to tears when I think of the terror and despair I suffered as a child and the goodness of God that is flowing into my life now.

There are Proverbs to provide wisdom; the four gospels of Matthew, Mark, Luke, and John to tell of the life and ministry of Jesus; Paul's letters to help shape a believer's theology; and so much more. There are stories in the Bible that can help guide your own life story. I read a little every day, and it helps me stay connected to the Lord.

There are so many benefits to being a child of God. He is your heavenly Father now, and you can take all your cares and worries and give them to Him! You can pray for your loved ones and yourself and know that He hears your prayers and will answer, although not always in the way you expect. Sometimes patience is needed, but He will answer. He will provide for you. You can make an affirmation list of scriptures from the Bible and repeat them often so that you will remember and believe. You can take your sins to Him and ask Him for forgiveness and help and know that with your repentance, He will forget them. He is such a Good God!

You can rely on the Lord in times of trouble! He resides within you and is an ever-present source of refuge and strength. Just ask Him. He will not allow any more trial than you can bear. Count on it. He is so good to us! There are times He asks others to come to our rescue or aid. He is such a blessing in our lives.

God heals. Holy Spirit is ever at work in you helping you become more like Jesus, and healing occurs in you as a result of His working in you. You can also ask Him yourself for healing, and He will draw you to the healing you need. Some churches have healing ministries where people can go for hands-on healing. There are inner healing ministries like Sozo and HeartSync Ministries. Some churches have prayer ministers available to pray with you after the service. Some churches have telephone prayer ministries where you can call and leave your request for healing for others to pray for you. There are many paths to receiving healing from God. You have your part to play as well. You need to identify a need and be willing to receive help. Sometimes patience is needed, as healing can be a process and not immediate. God's intention is always to heal.

You also have Holy Spirit who comforts you in times of need. Just ask. God's peace is ever available to you and a real blessing. It can come unbidden or you can ask for it. In addition, if you are willing to slow down long enough to listen and attend, the Lord will provide physical and emotional rest for your soul. He is such a good God!

You can learn to speak in tongues by being baptized in the Holy Spirit. Tongues is a spiritual language that allows you to speak directly to God. Although you don't know the meaning of the words, God does. Speaking in tongues allows you to stay connected with God, especially in times of trouble. It is such a comfort to have this gift.

God has many promises and blessings in store for you if you will become His child and be willing to receive them. You can find these promises in the Bible. Don't forget to honor and acknowledge Him and thank Him for His many blessings!

I used to believe that most everyone goes to heaven; after reading the Bible, I no longer believe that. Since God made this world, the world operates on His ideas, not mine. Just because I want everyone to go to heaven does not mean that will happen. I accepted that wisdom because He is God, and I am not. It has been easier for me since I surrendered my will to Him.

Life is process, and being Christian is a process like no other. It is God's grace that saves us, but we need to have faith in His son Jesus and BELIEVE in order to walk the Christian walk. Once you say the Salvation Prayer, God's Holy Spirit will guide you, but you need to do your part. Your part includes paying attention to the Holy Spirit and following Him, reading God's Word in the Bible, attending a believing church, and fellowshipping with other Christians. It is not difficult as long as you are committed to following His way and willing to be obedient. It depends on what you want. Living with Him changes you and changes your life. It is not always easy, but there is much joy and LIFE IS GOOD!!!

2. Walking It Out

Once you become a Christian, you start walking with God. Holy Spirit works with each believer in ways unique to that person. How He works with me is different from how He might work with you. That said, I want to provide insight by writing about how He has worked with me over the last several years.

I attended an outside speaker event at Faith Worship Center and sat next to a woman who told me about Iona, a tiny island in the Inner Hebrides off Scotland. The island is considered to be a "thin place" (close to heaven vibrationally) where the voice of Holy Spirit can easily be heard. Later, Holy spirit asked me if I wanted to go to Iona. Did I ever! I made plans to attend for a week the following June with a group of Christians from other countries. Our focus would be on peace and social justice.

I am certain Holy Spirit "planted" me next to that woman so I would hear about Iona. He knew I would be needing a real uplift after my spouse asked for a divorce in April of 2017—without actually using the word "divorce." He told me that he was moving in with his daughter to care for her and that it would also be a trial separation for us. He moved out soon thereafter with no notice. It was a pretty intense time for me. Although his behavior had been trying for quite some time, it was still quite difficult to actually acknowledge the reality of divorce and take the appropriate steps. I was attending the second year of Faith School of Supernatural Ministry at Faith Worship Center at the time. Leslie Russell, the advisor for my small group, helped me so much to cope with the divorce. I did get to Iona, loved it, and was able to accept my sexuality there; accepting my sexuality was a very big deal for me.

In early July, I spent several weeks at my sister's camp on Cold Stream Pond thoroughly cleaning it in anticipation of my family vacationing there. On my last day, Holy Spirit nudged me to head to the dock. At some point a kayaker named George Stevens paddled up and started talking about life. He was Christian and had lost his wife of many years to cancer. When he asked me if I were married, I told him my story. Later I thought about whether I could be reconciled to the man to whom I was married. I realized the marriage was over. I then made plans to see the new friend as an acquaintance, not as a date.

The divorce experience was most unpleasant. Holy Spirit made it difficult for me to think as I normally can so that I could learn to TRUST Him. I do trust Him now with my life, and it came about because of what He accomplished in me through the divorce process.

Holy Spirit encouraged me. He told me to call out to Jesus first thing in the morning to set the tone for the day. And I did. He told me He would provide for me and take care of me and not to worry. He told me the divorce wouldn't be pretty once my spouse realized I would fight. He told me He would tell me what to do. And He did. He coached me and cared for me. He helped me grow up in a hurry under terrible pressure since I wasn't able to function as I normally can. He worked through others to support me when I needed it most.

In December of 2018, George helped me to surrender deeply to God. In January, somehow God took my abilities so that I could learn to trust Him. God then sent His man George (who lived in Maine and I in Massachusetts) to help keep my spirits up, pray with me, take me out to dinner, and to support me in general. At God's request, George truly poured himself into my life. As Christians we were celibate and stayed that way until we later married. Holy Spirit brought George into my life and worked with each of us over time to prepare us for a future life together. How amazing is that?

I needed two divorce lawyers and a great deal of help to get through the divorce. My son Bailey offered to let me rent his townhouse at his cost, as I had no clue where I would go once the townhouse where I was living was sold. He also offered to help a number of times, helped me see that I needed a more experienced lawyer, and helped me work through some financial options. My daughter Heidi helped me plan what to do with my stuff and supported me emotionally as well.

My friend Joyce Graves prayed for me. She told me to pray in tongues at least an hour a day—preferably all day—and that a shield of faith would surround me. She told me that God had opened a door for a place for me to live! She gave me Ephesians 3:20 and Habakkuk 3:17-19 as scriptural support to pray over myself to keep me in a good place emotionally:

> Ephesians 3:20
>
> 20 Now to him who is able to do immeasurably more than all we ask or imagine, according to his power that is at work within us, (NIV)
>
> Habakkuk 3:17-19
>
> 17 Though the fig tree does not blossom and there is no fruit on the vines, [though] the product of the olive fails and the fields yield no food, though the flock is cut off from the fold and there are no cattle in the stalls,
>
> 18 Yet I will rejoice in the Lord; I will exult in the [victorious] God of my salvation!
>
> 19 The Lord God is my Strength, my personal bravery, and my invincible army; He makes my feet like hinds' feet and will make me to walk [not to stand still in terror, but to walk] and make [spiritual]

progress upon my high places [of trouble, suffering, or responsibility]! (AMP)

(Note from Joyce Meyer: "A hind is a type of mountain goat that can leap about freely on the rocky, difficult slopes. Hinds climb mountains with seemingly no effort at all because of the way God has made them."[9])

My friend Walter Niederberger prayed for me as well. On March 11, 2018, he heard words from the Holy Spirit for me:

You have a nice home

You will feel home

I will be comfortable

Safe and happy

A place to live and rejoice

Nicely furnished!

What a relief! Peace flooded my soul when I heard that. Walter continued to pray for me, and his prayers brought me much comfort and peace.

So many miracles came about through others: George, Bailey, Heidi, Leslie, Joyce, Walter, others too—all God's people. Where I couldn't, they could! God is so good.

On April 20, I came back to life, and my perspective returned as well. All fell into place. George readied the townhouse to sell. My former husband and I divorced May 8, 2018. The townhouse sold above the selling price after the open house. On July 29, 2018, somehow the belief that I was ugly was healed in the prayer room at

[9] The Everyday Life Bible Amplified Version Featuring Notes and Commentary by Joyce Meyer (New York, Boston, Nashville: Warner Faith, 2006) 1433.

Faith Worship Center. It evaporated into thin air! The parlor grand piano went for minor work and then to a museum. The divorce became final early August of 2018. Bailey and Heidi helped George and me sell remaining unneeded items and helped us move all of the things not already carted to Maine by George. The four of us celebrated a truly remarkable journey at George's beach house near the coast of Maine. Miracle after miracle. GOD IS GOOD!

August 26, 2018 in front of our beach home on our wedding day! GOD IS GOOD!

In August of 2018, George and I were married by his pastor and a few friends in a simple ceremony in the field in which his beach house sits. We started married life together knowing that God would work with each of us as the architect of our marriage. What an incredible blessing it is to have Holy Spirit speak to each believer and guide the way!

On August 20, 2019, at a favorite beach on Mount Desert Island, we heard from Holy Spirit: "I am restoring what Satan stole from you." Eureka!!! Talk about the goodness of God! Not long after that, we headed to Pemaquid Beach where I had worked as a teenager for several summers. Holy Spirit brought to mind many things for me to forgive that were long forgotten. One scenario was the time I was taken to a hospital where I was put in stirrups after I started bleeding. The doctor was shocked at what he found when he examined me: my dad had put things in me to stretch me and hurt me, and I had no conscious awareness of it. The doctor then dismissed me as being a slut.

Holy Spirit told me that Jesus was holding my hand throughout that terrible experience. He wants this in the book because people need to learn not to judge others. After that experience, I carried the feeling of being a slut—which I was not—and the shame of feeling that deep down until 2019 when I gave it to God!

In October of 2019 while George and I enjoyed lunch by a lighthouse, Holy Spirit brought to mind the incredible afternoon I had spent listening to someone speak about the times he had helped others by clearing them of trauma. I have always wanted to help others, and I was fascinated by his talk, especially since I knew nothing myself of trauma (at least not in the clinical sense). When it was needed, Holy Spirit reminded me of the experience, and soon after, the person who had helped others helped someone I cared about very deeply. Holy Spirit wants this in the book:

God has it all worked out!!! We need to trust Him and not try to do things in our own strength.

I don't think I was even born again at this time in my life, so that means Holy Spirit is at work in everyone's life whether born again or not. He is an incredibly beautiful person. *Thank you, Holy Spirit!*

That same month, our Pastor, Quinton Self, asked each person in the congregation of Anchor Church to ask themselves the following questions in the quiet time after the sermon:

Holy Spirit will you speak to me today?

Holy Spirit will you show me any unforgiveness in my soul?

I asked myself those questions and heard from Holy Spirit that He wanted me to love myself as much as He loves me and that He wanted me to honor myself. I asked Him how, and He told me to just start and He would show me. I found a video on YouTube on how to honor yourself, and I have made changes. I give myself permission to be me and others permission to be them. I can still laugh at myself and enjoy some of my quirks, but I do now honor who He made me to be. Thank you, Holy Spirit!

Several months later in November, I realized that I was actually beginning to care for myself, and caring for yourself is truly life-changing because you will then take the necessary steps. A few days later, I got healed from sadness long held from having had two miscarriages. The healing came to me in an unexpected way—through a prayer for women who had had an abortion. The prayer was from an Andrew Wommack CD loaned to me by my son. I had miscarriages, not an abortion, but evidently carried similar feelings. Peace came, and it was sweet.

The Holy spirit has continued to work with us to guide us and help us grow spiritually. We are currently restoring an old camp on Cold Stream Pond and learning to work together in the process. We are in our late seventies, full of life and energy, and ever hopeful for our future and the future of our loved ones. God is GOOD!!!

Epilogue

This material on spiritual practices is taken from my integrative paper, "Coming to Terms with Incest - Adult Survivors," written for my master's degree from Andover Newton Theological School (now Andover Newton Seminary at Yale Divinity School):

Spiritual Practices

I can only speak about my own practice of spirituality: it has changed me, it has helped me become more fully alive, it has changed my perspective on life. The experience of incest is a kind of death. Once the experience is over, the child must continue to deaden the self not to be overwhelmed by the feelings and to keep it secret in order to survive. Children who are threatened and tortured become expert at living half dead lives. That was my experience.

It can take tremendous courage to peek out from behind the wall of self-protection and many years of effort to transition from half dead to fully alive. Spiritual practices can aid in that transition, and I hope to help other survivors find practices to aid their transition. One that particularly helped me was the practice of *acceptance and surrender*, of saying yes to life. It allows self-acceptance, acceptance that the past cannot be changed but ways of looking at it can, letting go of the past, acceptance of the reality of God's love, letting go of the belief that one is now "spoiled goods" and robbed of life, and turning over one's life to God. There was a moment in my own life when I knew I couldn't go on as I was, so I surrendered to God. I found that the act of surrender is not a onetime event, but truly a process that can be aided by spiritual practices. I have actively sought healing and looked for truth and learned that God loves me as His precious child. Surrendering to His loving care has made all the difference. Surrender and acceptance become a way of life that feeds life.

Another practice, the practice of *Sabbath* has real implications for my ministry for incest survivors for them as well as for myself. Incest is a tough issue. A Sabbath of any duration can provide a much-needed change of focus as well as nourishment, refuge, and perspective. Sabbath moments of affirmation and prayer and Sabbath walks in the beauty of the natural world can provide a break from the intensity of past experience. Even placing one flower in a vase on a desk can invite the real world into a life; taking five minutes to really look at a beautiful picture can provide Sabbath nourishment.

Many other spiritual practices can be embraced in the process of becoming more fully alive: The practice of *gratitude* or deep thankfulness can put our focus where it belongs and off us and remind us to stay positive, a happier way to live. *Worship* allows the expression of gratitude for who God is and what He has done in our life and in the lives of our loved ones. *Prayer* - especially prayer guided by the Holy Spirit - changes things and empowers us to believe we are part of the process of life. *Centering Prayer*, a method of silent prayer, is a practice that deepens relationship with God and is available as a source of comfort when needed. *Play* brings perspective to life and the sense we are okay and all is well. *Forgiveness* of self and others keeps us free from being chained to others and allows openness for more of the joy of life. The practice of *lament* can help us move the sludge of life out of the way and find peace. Finally, *listening* to life and to the Holy Spirit provides a way of knowing what is being asked of us.

My Dream of Helping Others

"Let us not lose heart in doing good, for in due time we will reap if we do not grow weary." Galatians 6:9 (NASB)

Double rainbow at Cold Stream Pond.

Take a close look at this photo taken at Cold Stream Pond, the scene of many happy family times. Do you see the double rainbow? Now what does a double rainbow have to do with losses? It makes me think of a certain song:

> Somewhere over the rainbow
>
> Skies are blue
>
> And the dreams that you dare to dream
>
> Really do come true.

And the dream that I have is that the experiences of my childhood that have brought so many losses will also bring gains. Out of my losses can come help and healing and wholeness for others; as a wounded healer, I can be an authentic agent of healing because I have been there. By my being willing to stand as an incest survivor, I am hopeful that others will be encouraged to stand and that together we can bring change to help remove the scourge of evil that is incest.

About the Author

Lynne Stevens has always had a passion in her heart to help others. In her book, *Look What God Can Do,* she shares painful experiences from her childhood in the hope that others will be encouraged to find their own way to the goodness of God. If she can make it to that wonderful life God intends, so can the reader!

She has always loved to write—first, little childhood books; later, computer programs, papers as an English major and as a theology student, and an e-book *From Incest to Hope: how to heal the pain and find joy in the process.* Her voice is an authentic one, as she has endured much.

Her goals in publishing this book include bringing as many people to Jesus as possible, bringing hope to incest survivors and others, helping fund a rose covered beach cottage where an incest survivor can heal, and become the Heidi Baker for incest survivors.

Lynne is married and shares with her spouse a home and a camp both in Maine. She has two children and their spouses, three grandchildren, and extended family as well. She received her bachelor's degree in English with a minor in psychology from the University of Maine and her Master of Arts in Theological Studies at Andover Newton Theological School (now Andover Newton Seminary at Yale Divinity School). Her focus was pastoral ministry especially as it related to incest. She graduated from two years of the Faith School of Supernatural Ministry (FSSM) taught at Faith Worship Center, Pepperell, MA.